PARENTING PRE-SCHOOL CHILDREN

D1388625

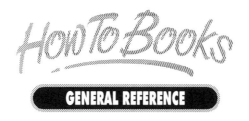

GENERAL REFERENCE

PARENTING PRE-SCHOOL CHILDREN

How to cope with common
behavioural problems

Paul Stallard

I'VE LEARNED THREE NEW WORDS TODAY!

How To Books

Cartoons by Mike Flanagan

British Library Cataloguing in Publication Data
A catalogue record for this book is available from the British Library.

First published in 1998 by How To Books Ltd, 3 Newtec Place,
Magdalen Road, Oxford, OX4 1RE, United Kingdom.
Tel: (01865) 793806. Fax: (01865) 248780.

Note: The material contained in this book is set out in good faith for
general guidance and no liability can be accepted for loss or expense
incurred as a result of relying in particular circumstances on statements
made in this book. The law and regulations may be complex and liable to
change, and readers should check the current position with the relevant
authorities before making personal arrangements.

Produced for How To Books by Deer Park Productions.
Typeset by Concept Communications Ltd, Crayford, Kent.
Printed and bound by Cromwell Press, Trowbridge, Wiltshire.

Contents

List of Illustrations

Preface

Being a parent is probably the most important task you will ever undertake and yet it is a job for which most parents feel totally unprepared. There is no formal training and parents are simply expected to know how to help their children learn to behave. It is therefore not surprising that many regularly question what they are doing and doubt and worry about their ability to be good parents.

Despite these worries the majority of parents do a very good job. They provide their children with opportunities and encouragement to learn new skills and teach them how to behave well. However, the range of skills that children have to learn during the pre-school years is enormous and inevitably there will be some things that just don't seem to go right.

This book is written for parents, carers and child care professionals and offers both reassurance and step-by-step advice about how to cope with common difficulties. It emphasises a positive approach and provides many ideas about how problems can be prevented and how children can be encouraged to behave well. The most common pre-school difficulties of sleeping, eating, toileting and coping with tempers and defiance are discussed in depth and many practical suggestions are provided.

Paul Stallard

DOES YOUR CHILD?

Wake during the night   Wet themself during the day

Have a very small appetite

Refuse to do as you ask   Only pooh in their nappy

Refuse to go to bed

Hold on until the last minute to use the toilet   Eat only a few foods

Shout or hit you if you tell them off

Pooh or wet their pants   Sleep in your bed

Refuse to try any new foods

Ignore you   Have nightmares

Become constipated

Need you with them to settle at night   Have lots of tempers

Seem to need very little sleep

Mess around at mealtimes   Only eat 'junk' food

Refuse to pooh on the toilet

Be unkind to other children   Eat snacks but not meals

Behave for everyone else but not for you

Keep shouting out at bedtime   Eat very slowly

Show you up in public

Have lots of daytime naps   Throw themselves to the floor in rage

Seem afraid to use the toilet

Drink lots but eat little   Wake up early in the morning

1
Learning to Behave

HOW CHILDREN LEARN TO BEHAVE

Parenting children is a complicated and demanding task for which most parents feel untrained and unprepared. Parents are expected to provide their children with:

- good physical care and protection from danger

- love, affection and social approval

- play, stimulation and teaching to help them learn

- opportunities and encouragement to become independent so they are more able to accept responsibility.

Another important task of a parent is to help their children learn how to behave well. Most of what a child does is learned and the range of skills a child has to master during the pre-school years is enormous. They include how to:

- crawl and walk

- use and understand speech

- sleep, feed themselves, and use the toilet

- play on their own and co-operate with other children

- count, identify colours, understand written words.

Children learn these skills over time either by being taught or by watching and copying others. As well as learning skills, children also learn how to behave and they learn what behaviour is acceptable and what is not. This is a difficult and complex task and it is not surprising that sometimes problems arise. This can happen when children:

- learn unacceptable behaviour

- have few opportunities to learn to behave well

- learn that misbehaving gets them what they want.

Learning unacceptable behaviour

In the same way that children learn to behave well, they can also learn to misbehave. They can pick up bad habits.

- If they hear their parents use bad language they may copy it thinking that these words are acceptable.

- If children see their parents shout and throw things during an argument they may learn that this is what you do when you get angry.

In these situations children may copy inappropriate behaviour and learn to swear or throw things when they get angry.

Having few opportunities to learn to behave well

In order to learn, children need opportunities to practise. For some, opportunities may be limited, resulting in children failing to learn how to behave or develop new skills.

- An only child who is isolated with no friends or relatives will have few opportunities to learn how to play with other children.

- A child who is kept in nappies will not learn to use the potty.

In these situations problems may arise because the children have few opportunities to learn and practise what to do.

Learning that misbehaving gets them what they want

The third common reason why children may not behave well is that they learn that their misbehaviour results in some sort of benefit.

- Children may learn that having a temper tantrum in a shop results in their parents buying sweets to calm them down.

- They may learn that if they ignore their parents they can do as they wish.

In these situations children may learn that their behaviour has advantages. They have learned to have tempers and to ignore their parents.

Situations and consequences

Children do not usually misbehave all the time. How a child behaves is affected by:

- the situation in which they find themselves; and

- the consequences that follow their behaviour.

BEHAVING DIFFERENTLY IN DIFFERENT SITUATIONS

Parents often find that their children behave differently depending upon who they are with, where they are, the time of day and what they are doing.

Who are they with?

Children learn that different people have different rules and react to the same behaviour in different ways.

- A child may have constant temper tantrums with one parent but none with the other. This may be because one parent is firm and ignores their outbursts whilst the other gives in for a 'quiet life'.

People also require children to do different things.

- children may play happily at their grandparents where there are few pressures and they are allowed to do as they wish. With their parents, deadlines have to be met, daily life organised, jobs completed, and this may result in more demands on the children and frequent tempers.

Where are they?

Children will behave differently depending upon where they are.

- Children may be very uncooperative at home with their parents and yet be very compliant if they go out shopping or on special trips.

- At playgroup, children may play very contentedly with the toys but at home be constantly wanting their parents' attention.

What is the day and time?

It is not uncommon to find times or days throughout the week which are either particularly good or bad.

- A child may be content and settled during the morning but become unhappy and unsettled for the hour before tea each night.

- Weekdays may be very difficult but at weekends the child is happy, content and does as they are asked.

What are they doing?
Often children are better behaved when they do certain activities.

● A child may be active and unable to concentrate if you read them a story but can sit down for thirty minutes playing with their building bricks or painting.

● A child on their own may end up bored and misbehaving but when you play with them they are happy and co-operative.

UNDERSTANDING THE CONSEQUENCES OF BEHAVIOUR

The other important point to consider is what happens after children behave in a certain way, i.e. what are the consequences of what they do. For each behaviour there is a consequence:

Behaviour		Consequence
Saying 'I love you'	results in	a smile and a hug
Sitting on the toilet	results in	parent saying, 'well done'
Hitting sister	results in	sister crying, TV turned off
Ignoring parent	results in	'doing what I want to do'
Having a tantrum	results in	being ignored

Sometimes consequences are seen by children to be nice and result in them getting something they want or like. If consequences are seen by children to be pleasant, then this will increase the chance that they will behave that way again.

● If they enjoy a smile and a hug they will be more likely to say 'I love you' again.

● If they like your attention then they may be more likely to sit on the toilet again.

On other occasions, the consequences might be unpleasant and result in something happening to the child that they do not like or want. If the consequences are seen by the child to be unpleasant, this will reduce the chance that they will behave that way again.

● If a child does not like the TV being turned off, they will be less likely to hit their sister again.

● If they do not like being ignored, they will be less likely to have frequent or long tantrums.

Learning that consequences vary

On some occasions children find that their behaviour results in a number of different consequences. Some of these may be seen by the child to be pleasant whereas others are unpleasant.

Behaviour	*Consequence*
Tim jumping on the furniture	Mum tells Tim off
	Gran tells mum off and gives Tim a sweet

Whilst Tim may not like being told off by his mother, his jumping on the furniture has resulted in a sweet which he enjoys. Tim will probably be confused and unsure whether jumping on furniture is really unacceptable.

What happens will also vary depending on how consistent the adults are.

Behaviour	*Consequences*
Lee snatched a toy	With dad, made to give the toy back
	With mum, she is ignored

Lee will be confused and unsure whether snatching toys is an acceptable or unacceptable way of getting what she wants.

Using the consequence rules

Parents can help children clearly and quickly learn what is acceptable and what is not by using the consequence rules.

1. Make sure that the child receives no positive consequences for misbehaving. This will clearly show the child that misbehaviour does not result in any positive benefits.

2. Make sure that the child receives lots of positive consequences for behaving well. This will help the child learn that positive behaviour is noticed and results in nice things.

3. Make the consequences as consistent as possible. This will help the child learn that the consequences are always the same, regardless of where they are or who is around.

4. Make sure that the consequences are immediate. This will help the child learn the link between how they behaved and the consequences.

Gaining attention

One of the most powerful influences on the behaviour of young children is the amount of parental attention they receive. Young children often like their parents' attention and work out ways in which they can get it. Unfortunately, parents are not always very good at noticing or praising their children when they behave well. Typically parents react and comment when children misbehave. A number of children therefore learn that they get noticed when they play up.

Being told off is not usually thought of by parents as being something that children like. Whilst this may be the case it is not so much what you say but the fact that they have managed to gain your undivided attention. Their misbehaviour has succeeded in getting them noticed.

Using the attention rule

Children need and want the attention of their parents. It is important that they receive it but make sure that:

1.   they get attention when they behave well

2.   misbehaviour is ignored and results in little attention.

UNDERSTANDING YOUR CHILD'S BEHAVIOUR

To understand how your child behaves, firstly decide what you are particularly interested in finding out about. Try and be as specific as you can and avoid general labels like 'being good'. This usually means many different things so it is best to focus on one particular aspect such as:

● temper tantrums

● mealtime behaviour

● waking up at night

● toileting accidents

● hitting other children.

Keeping a diary

Once you are clear what you are looking for, keep a short diary for a week or two and write down every time this happens. Using the following headings in your diary will help you understand how and why your child behaves as they do. Write down:

● the day and time it happened

● what was going on just before it happened, who was there, what they were doing

- what exactly your child did

- how you dealt with it.

Keeping your diary in this way will help you discover:

- how often your child behaves this way

- whether this happens at specific times or on certain days of the week

- what else is going on to 'trigger' this behaviour

- whether it only happens with certain people

- how you react.

Example: Zara's tantrum

Zara was thirty months and had recently started to have lots of temper tantrums. She had always had temper outbursts but recently her parents, Joe and Sue, thought that these were becoming worse and more frequent. They decided to keep a diary for a week to find out more. An extract from the diary is shown in Figure 1.

Day and time	What was happening?	What did Zara do?	What did we do?
Monday 9.30am	Zara was watching TV. Told her that it was time to get dressed.	Zara threw herself to the ground, crying.	Told her not to be silly. Promised to play a game with her and after 10 minutes she was OK.
11.00am	Zara asked for a biscuit. Refused.	Cried and screamed for 5 minutes.	Gave a biscuit to calm her down.
1.40pm	Zara wanted to watch TV. Told her to play with her dolls.	Zara threw herself to the floor and screamed.	Ignored her but after 5 minutes promised her a video if she calmed down.
5.00pm	Asked Zara to come and sit at the table for tea.	Zara said no. Cried and said wanted tea in front of TV.	Agreed she could have a sandwich and watch the TV.
6.30pm	Joe told Zara that it was bedtime.	Zara said No. Cried for 10 minutes.	Ignored her. She sat quietly on the settee and by 7.05 was asleep.

Fig. 1. Zara's temper diary.

This day from Zara's diary was fairly typical. Zara was having about five tempers each day during which she would scream and cry. There did not appear to be any pattern to these tempers. They could happen at any time and with both parents, although Joe and Sue noticed that most of the tempers happened if Zara was unable to get her own way. Joe and Sue were surprised to find how they dealt with these tempers and learned that they nearly always gave in to her. The diary helped Sue and Joe understand that Zara had learned that tantrums were a good way of getting what she wanted.

'I still can't understand what made my child behave like that'
There will be times when a diary still doesn't help you understand why your child behaves as they do. This happened for Djemal's parents who were trying to understand why their son was unkind to other children at nursery. They kept a diary for a week and recorded the two incidents detailed in Figure 2

Day and time	What was happening?	What did Djemal do?	What did you do?
Monday 11.00	Sitting down with all other children at story time.	Pushed Tom off his seat.	Sent him to sit on his own for 2 minutes.
Thursday 9.40	Just started painting with three other children.	Painted over Bob's picture.	Sent him away from painting table for 2 minutes.

Fig. 2. Djemal's 'being unkind' diary

The consequences for this unkindness were clear and Djemal did not seem to gain anything positive by his misbehaviour. It seemed that these incidents were unprovoked and that Djemal had just decided to be unkind. This didn't seem to make sense to his parents since Djemal was not like this anywhere else. He was often caring and considerate of other children, playing and sharing toys well.

The nursery staff decided to keep a careful watch on Djemal. They noticed that Djemal had toys snatched off him, was called unkind names and that he was sometimes kicked, particularly by Tom and Bob. Djemal did not retaliate when this happened but at a later date he usually got his own back. Djemal's unkind behaviour was now making sense.

If the diary does not help you understand why your child is behaving as they do, try thinking about what happened earlier in the day. Often you will find a reason.

CASE STUDIES

Mike has accidents

Mike was dry and clean during the day by the age of three. When Mike was four his family moved house and he started to have toileting accidents again. His parents decided to keep a diary to try and find out more about why these were happening. Part of his diary is shown in Figure 3.

Day and time	What was happening?	What did Mike do?	What did we do?
Monday 9.30	Getting ready to leave the house.	Wet his pants.	Calmly changed him.
Monday 9.45	Arrived at nursery saying goodbye.	Pooed himself.	Took him home to change.
Wednesday 9.25	Just left house to walk to nursery.	Pooed himself.	Changed him.
Monday 9.40	Arrived at nursery.	Wet his pants.	Took clean pair of pants to nursery so quickly changed him.

Fig. 3. Mike's 'accident' diary.

The diary showed that Mike only had accidents when he went to nursery. Mike's parents talked with him about nursery and found that he was being teased by another boy. They talked about this with the nursery staff who arranged for Mike to play with some other children as soon as he arrived. After two weeks Mike went off to nursery happily and had no more accidents.

Jacob reacts to inconsistent consequences

Jacob had recently started at playgroup and was not getting on very well with the other children. He was snatching toys and hitting other children if he could not get his own way. The playgroup staff and his mother decided to find out more about what was going on and kept a diary for a few days. An extract from the diary is shown in Figure 4.

The diary showed that Jacob was being aggressive to the other children although there did not seem to be a particular pattern as to when or with whom it would happen. The consequences of his aggression varied and sometimes Jacob would get what he wanted (positive consequences) whilst at other times he would have to say sorry, return what he had taken, or be sent to sit on his own (negative consequences). Having recognised this, Jacob's mother and the playgroup staff agreed how they would deal with any aggression in a consistent way. They made sure that the consequences for aggression were always negative.

Day and time	What was happening?	What did Jacob do?	What did we do?
Monday 9.40	Jacob playing cars with Tom.	Snatched car from Tom.	Told Jacob to say sorry.
10.05	Walking around on his own.	Pushed Kelly off the pedal car.	Told Jacob that it was wrong to hurt others. Gave the car to Kelly.
10.45	Painting with Luke and Sara.	Snatched the paints from Luke.	Ignored him.
10.50	Got down from painting.	Took football from Tom.	Ignored him.
11.25	Listening to story.	Kicked Sara.	Told him that this was naughty. Sent him to sit on his own.

Fig. 4. Jacob's playgroup diary.

What did we ask?	What did Katy do?
Katy was playing in her bedroom. Called her to come for breakfast.	Ignored me. Carried on playing in her room.
Told Katy to come otherwise she would miss her breakfast.	Katy came down.
Asked Katy to go upstairs and get her shoes.	Katy put her shoes on.
Asked Katy to brush her teeth.	Katy brushed her teeth.
Asked Katy to put her toys away.	Carried on playing in her room.
Asked her again to put her toys away.	Carried on playing in her room.
Told her that we would not go out until she tidied up.	Came downstairs and picked up her toys.
Asked Katy to get her coat on.	Put her coat on.
Returned from being out. Told her to take her bag upstairs.	Took bag upstairs.
Asked Katy to help tidy her bedroom.	Came upstairs with me and helped tidy.

Fig. 5. Katy's diary.

Katy's diary

Katy was a strong-willed girl who was often determined to have her own way. Her parents felt that she never did a thing they asked and so decided to check this out. They recorded what happened the next ten times they asked Katy to do something (see Figure 5).

The diary showed that although Katy sometimes ignored her parents, it was not as bad as they had thought. Out of the ten requests they made, Katy immediately did as she was asked on seven occasions. The diary helped her parents get things in perspective and recognise those times when she did as she was asked.

DISCUSSION POINTS

1. Write down all the good things your child has done today and think how often you have praised them for behaving well. How could you make sure that you praised more of their good behaviour?

2. Think about the last time your child played up. Write down in detail what happened. How could you make sure that they received no positive consequences or attention for behaving this way?

3. Are there any times when your child is more likely to misbehave? What do you think are the reasons for this?

2
Helping Children to Behave Well

POSITIVE PARENTING SKILLS

How a parent reacts to a child who is behaving well or deals with a child who is misbehaving is important and will affect their child's future behaviour. Some parenting skills are more likely to encourage children to behave well and the following five have been found to be particularly important.

1. Clear rules which are consistently enforced

Children who have parents with clear rules which are firmly and fairly enforced have been found to be better behaved. If the rules are vague or occasionally overlooked then children become confused and will not know when to take their parents seriously.

2. Good parental monitoring

Parents need to monitor what their children do. Potentially dangerous situations need to be quickly stopped. Misbehaviour needs to be checked and corrected at an early stage. Requests have to be followed through to ensure that the child has done as requested. Children with fewer behaviour problems have parents who are better at supervising their children.

3. Consistent management

The way in which a parent praises good behaviour and deals with misbehaviour is important. The more consistent the parents, the more predictable the children's world and the quicker they will learn the consequences of their behaviour. If the consequences are inconsistent, children may become confused. The reaction they receive depends more on luck or how the parent is feeling rather than on clear rules.

4. Praise for good behaviour

Parents of children with behaviour problems have been found to ignore or praise less of their children's good or positive behaviour. Typically this gets overlooked and the children receive little parental attention or praise for behaving well. These children learn that playing up gets them noticed. Being good gets them ignored.

5. Punishment

Children with behaviour problems often have parents who are more extreme in their use of punishment. Their parents will be more likely to both threaten and carry out punishment if their child misbehaves and over time the punishment often becomes more severe.

The results of this and other work begins to help parents understand how they can parent their children in ways that are less likely to create problems. These ideas are not guaranteed and there will be many times when they do not immediately work. However, over time they will undoubtedly be beneficial and will help your child learn to behave well.

SETTING FIRM AND PREDICTABLE LIMITS

Families have many rules about what is permitted and what is not allowed. Some rules will be shared by many families; for example:

- you do not hit other people
- you play nicely with other children
- you do as you are asked.

Other rules will vary between families; for example:

- you sit at the table to eat your meal
- you go to bed by 7.00pm each night
- you say sorry if you do something wrong.

For many families the rules are not always clear.

- Partners may have different rules. One partner may insist that their child is in bed by 7.30 whilst the other may prefer a later bedtime.
- Rules may vary between days. A child may be allowed to sleep in their parents' bed when their father is on the night shift, but not when he is on the day shift.
- Rules may vary depending on how you are feeling. If you are tense and wound up your children may be told off about things which on a better day would be overlooked.

- Rules are not always clearly stated. People usually expect children to behave in certain ways but often this is not made clear to the children. Often children find out what is expected of them when they have done wrong and get told off.

Agreeing clear rules

To make everyday life clear for you and your child it is important to agree upon the rules of the family.

- Choose a small number of 'golden rules'. These rules should be about those things you consider to be the most important. Limit the number of golden rules and be prepared to live with some of your child's irritating although less important misbehaviour.

- Write your rules down and put them up in the kitchen or some other convenient place. This will prevent any confusion, aid consistency between partners and remind you about what you have agreed.

Enforce the rules consistently

Having clear rules is important but these rules will only help your child to behave well if they are consistently used. During the course of busy family life it is too easy for rules to get overlooked, conveniently forgotten or erratically used. Your 'golden rules' need to be enforced. Every time they are broken you need to ensure that your child receives a clear message that their behaviour is unacceptable.

GIVING CLEAR AND SIMPLE INSTRUCTIONS

Giving children clear, short instructions and using words they understand will help your children learn how you would like them to behave. Often parents use unnecessarily long or complicated instructions. They may provide endless explanations which become increasingly complex and leave children feeling confused.

When giving instructions to children it is important to remember the following six guidelines.

1. Start the instruction with the child's name and ask them to look at you

This simple procedure makes sure that your child knows that you are talking to them, and the chances of them listening to what you say are increased. If your child will not look at you, hold their head and put your face in front of theirs so that they have to look.

2. Give clear and short instructions

The chances of your child doing as you request will be increased if your instructions are clear. Ask your child to 'please put the bricks in the box' rather than 'tidy up the bricks', to 'hold your hand' rather than 'to behave'. Making the instruction very specific and short will help the child understand what they have to do and increases the chance that they will remember what you have said.

3. Use simple, single request instructions

It is often better to give children single rather than multiple request instructions. Asking them to 'put their toys in the box' and once that is done asking them to 'put their books on the table' is preferable to telling them to 'put their toys in the box and put their books on the table'. Multiple instructions may overwhelm or confuse them and will increase the chance that something will be forgotten.

4. Use positive commands

Parents often tell their children to stop doing things rather than telling them how to behave instead. This is a negative approach and wherever possible it should be avoided. Instead of saying to a child who is jumping on the furniture to 'stop messing around', try asking them to 'sit quietly on the settee'. Try asking the child who snatches toys from other children to 'share with Peter' rather than saying 'don't do that'. Wherever possible, use positive commands which tell children how you want them to behave.

5. Say it and mean it

The tone of your voice is as important as what you say. Often parents make weak or half-hearted requests which send a clear signal to their children that this request can be ignored. Sound determined, speak loudly and firmly and look as if you mean what you have said. There is no point trying to say something serious or important if you are smiling or laughing as you talk.

6. Physically back up the instruction if needed

Asking a child to do something only to be met by defiance is a common experience that leads parents to repeat themselves time and time again. On these occasions and at times when there is a potential danger to the child (e.g. picking up a kitchen knife) parents need to physically back up their instructions. The child who refuses to pick up their toys needs to be taken to them, their hand held and guided to pick them up. The knife needs to be removed before any damage can be done. This gives a clear signal to the child that you follow through what you say.

PREVENTING PROBLEMS

Young children need regular guidance and good supervision by their parents to:

- prevent accidents

- stop dangerous situations happening

- prevent naughty behaviour or difficult situations from escalating

- make sure that the children have done as they have been asked.

Supervision is time consuming and can be frustrating for parents who have to stop what they are doing to check on their children. Whilst this is frustrating it cannot be avoided. Unfortunately children are not born with a set of rules and a sense of danger and without careful monitoring they will undoubtedly get into mischief. Good supervision is required to prevent problems. If you are aware of problems beginning to build up then you may find the following strategies helpful.

Using distraction

A very useful technique, particularly with young children, is distraction. This is a way of stopping or preventing a child misbehaving by getting them to think about or do something else. You could try to distract:

- a toddler about to push something into the video machine by asking if they would like to come and help you get the washing in

- a child who keeps trying to touch electrical sockets by asking them to build you a model with their bricks

- a child who keeps trying to open a door by singing songs and dancing.

The distraction you choose will depend upon what you can think of and what your child likes doing. The idea is to encourage them to do something else so that they forget what they are doing. Distraction does not always work but it is a simple technique that is well worth trying.

Changing the routine

Sometimes you will find that difficult behaviour happens more often on certain days, at set times or when you do certain things. At these times you might want to try changing your routine and do things differently.

- If your child cries and runs off whenever you take them to playgroup, try arranging to walk with another parent and child.

- If your child is very unsettled in the morning when you are doing your jobs, try doing them in the afternoon when your child is more settled.

- If your child becomes very irritable for the hour before tea time, try arranging for tea to be slightly earlier.

Experiment, try and do things differently and see if a change in routine can prevent some difficult situations happening.

Breaking the cycle

There will be times when you will have difficult days. Your child may repeatedly misbehave or go from one tantrum to another. They may appear very unsettled or uninterested in playing and repeatedly end up in mischief. At these times it is useful to break this frustrating cycle by having a change of scene:

- Go to the shops.

- Go for a walk to post a letter.

- Visit a friend.

- Have a walk around the field.

Getting out and having a short change of scene is helpful because it:

- breaks into a very difficult situation and stops it continuing

- gives parents a chance to calm down and unwind

- provides the child with something else to do, look at and think about.

Quite often, staying at home on these days only makes the situation worse. Getting out gives everybody a break and often children seem more content when they return.

ENCOURAGING GOOD BEHAVIOUR

Prompting children to behave well

There are times when parents expect or know that their children will misbehave. Typically they watch and wait until their child plays up and then tell them off. An alternative, more positive approach is to encourage children to behave well.

- If your child usually runs off whilst shopping, ask them before you leave home to hold your hand.

- If your son often uses his fingers to eat his food, remind him to use his spoon when you give him his dinner.

- If your daughter regularly snatches toys from other children, ask her to tell you when she wants to play with something another child has.

This approach is positive and:

- gives a very clear message to your child how you would like them to behave

- gives you an opportunity to praise your child for behaving well rather than waiting to tell them off for misbehaving

- gives you an opportunity to say more good things about your child and ensures your child hears more positive messages

Praising good behaviour

The way a parent reacts to a child who behaves well is important. children need to learn that their good behaviour is:

- noticed,

- praised, and

- results in attention from adults.

Children like praise and attention from their parents and become expert at working out how they can obtain it. They quickly learn that behaving in certain ways is more likely to get them noticed. Unfortunately, parents are not always very good at praising their children. Many children learn that they get more attention for their misbehaviour. If this happens, it is likely that the children will continue to misbehave.

Is is therefore important for parents to praise their children when they have behaved well. Try and look for your children's good behaviour.

- Tell them that you have noticed. A short message is all that is needed; for example:
  'Thank you, Mike, for putting your toys away.'
  'You have eaten your meal nicely today, Helen.'
  'I am pleased you held my hand when we crossed the road, Tom.'
  'Well done, Rebecca, you went straight to bed when I asked.'

- Be specific in your comments since this emphasises to the child what they have done.

- Sound and look as if you are pleased.

Using behaviour charts

For children of three years and older, parents can use behaviour charts to encourage their children to behave well. These are simple ways of clearly signalling to your children that certain behaviours:

- are important

- will be encouraged

- get noticed.

For parents, the charts:

- help them remember what to look out for

- remind them to praise their children

- enable working parents and other important people to become more involved

- provide a record of how things are going.

Behaviour charts are very easy to set up and involve the following five steps.

What do you want your child to do?
Decide on what particular behaviour you want to encourage. Try and be specific and positive, i.e. 'hold mum's hand and stay with her when shopping' rather than 'not playing up when out'. This is your child's target.

Tell your child
Talk about this with your child. Tell them why the target is important,

how you want them to behave and what will happen. Be enthusiastic when talking since this will stir your child's interest and increase their motivation to try and behave well.

Make a chart
With your child make a special chart or draw a picture that is divided up into sections. Explain that every time they achieve their target they can either stick a star on their chart, draw on a smiley face or colour a piece of their picture. If they fail to earn their target then they receive no star or smiley face and do not colour in a piece of their picture. Examples of two charts are shown in Figure 6.

Adam's sitting on the potty chart
Each time Adam sits on the potty and tries to poo he earns one smiley face.

Wendy's going to bed chart
Wendy can colour in one part of her sleepy cat for going to bed when asked.

Fig. 6. Examples of behaviour charts

Praise them if they earn their target

If children earn their target, always make sure that you praise them, look pleased and talk about how well they have done. If they fail to earn their target, do not make a big fuss, provide them with little attention but remind them to try again next time. Always remember to make sure that they receive most attention for behaving well.

Decide when to start

Agree when the programme will start and remember to keep reminding your child about how you would like them to behave.

Using reward programmes

A child's motivation can be increased by linking behaviour charts to special rewards and treats. The treats are up to the parents to decide and could be anything including:

- activities such as going for a swim or to a special playground

- little toys

- extra things to eat such as sweets or ice creams

- doing something special with someone such as having tea at grandma's.

It is up to you whether you decide to link a behaviour chart to a reward programme and you need to weigh up the advantages and disadvantages.

Advantages	*Disadvantages*
Can increase a child's motivation to behave well	Child becomes materialistic and expects special treats for behaving well.
Often get quicker results.	Can be problems fading out the special treats.
Clear way of helping children learn that their behaviour affects what happens.	Child may want/expect bigger and bigger treats.

If you decide to use a reward programme, it is important to follow these guidelines:

- *You* decide what treats your child can earn. As a rule of thumb, doing something special with an adult is preferable to treats which involve money.

- Frequent, small treats are more effective than one-off very large treats, since they provide children with more of a sense of success and more opportunities to enjoy their special rewards.

- Make the treat earnable. Children have a limited understanding of time and number and setting a target of ten stars or fourteen days may be outside their level of comprehension.

- Always accompany any treat with lots of praise, hugs and attention.

COPING WITH MISBEHAVIOUR

The way parents deal with their child's misbehaviour is important. Providing too much attention to a child who plays up may teach them that misbehaving is a good way of getting noticed. Giving in to the demands of a crying child may teach them that crying is a good way of getting what they want. Giving in to a child who has long tempers may teach them that if they continue to make a fuss they will eventually get what they want.

Ignoring minor misbehaviour

Children do many things which are not acceptable or which seem to parents to be rude, inappropriate, unnecessary and very annoying. Many of these are relatively minor and picking your child up every time they happen may blow them up out of all proportion. This may:

- provide your child with unnecessary attention for misbehaving

- run the risk of a minor situation becoming worse

- teach your child that this misbehaviour gets them noticed

- make you feel that you are always telling your child off

- increase the number of critical comments your child hears.

In order to avoid this it is better to ignore any minor misbehaviour. This may be difficult and will probably need practice but it will help your child to learn that they get your attention when they behave well.

Dealing with major misbehaviour

Some things are more important and should not be ignored. On these occasions children need a clear message that what they have done is unacceptable and has a 'cost' to them.

Using the 'time out' method

One of the most effective ways of dealing with the more serious misbehaviour of children aged three years and older is by a method called 'time out'. This involves withdrawing your attention for a short time by sending the child to a particular place for a few minutes. This could be a special chair in the corner of a room, sitting on the bottom step of the stairs or sending them to their bedroom. You decide where you would like to use but make sure that it is safe and the child cannot damage themselves.

When your child misbehaves:

● Tell them simply and clearly that they have done wrong. 'Jane, you do not bite' or 'James, you do not throw toys'.

● Tell them firmly to go to 'time out'.

● If they refuse, repeat your request and if they still refuse physically take them.

● The child has to stay in 'time out' for a short period of time. Two minutes is usually long enough.

● Make sure they stay in 'time out' and if they get up and run around, firmly return them. Try to avoid talking or reasoning with them — this is not the right time.

● Repeat this procedure every time they misbehave.

What about smacking?

Some parents deal with their child's misbehaviour by giving them a smack. In many cases this is used as a last resort, often in desperation by frustrated parents who do not know what else to do. Although the rights and wrongs of smacking children will continue to be argued, a key question we need to consider is whether it is effective. The evidence to date would suggest that smacking does not work and may create future problems.

'Time out' is a more effective way of helping young children learn that their misbehaviour is unacceptable. It provides parents and children with time to calm down and this often prevents difficult situations from getting any worse. Finally it is a measured and controlled procedure that does not involve physical contact and so there is less danger that punishment will become more extreme.

CASE STUDIES

Sally's behaviour chart

Sally was three years old and had never been a good walker and would complain and cry if she had to walk anywhere. Her parents persisted but recently Sally had started throwing herself to the ground and refusing to move. This was embarrassing for her parents who often ended up picking her up and carrying her. They decided to try and encourage Sally to walk by using a behaviour chart.

Sally loved dogs and so her father drew a big picture of a Dalmatian puppy with lots of spots. Sally was told that she could colour in one spot every time she walked nicely when they went out. Before each outing she was reminded to try and earn another spot. During the outing her parents would make regular comments about how well she was doing. Upon returning home, if she walked her parents would praise her and Sally was allowed to colour in another spot. Sally was excited and very proud of her special chart and was keen to try and colour in her dog. Sally learned that she received more attention for behaving well and her walking improved.

Craig's reward programme

For five-year-old Craig, each morning started with a battle with his parents over getting dressed. Although he was perfectly able to dress himself, Craig refused. His parents had already tried a behaviour chart but Craig didn't seem interested and after a week they gave up. The battles seemed to be getting worse and they were often late taking his older sister to school.

Craig was very interested in animals. His parents decided to try a reward programme and talked with him about a visit to the local animal home if he got himself dressed in the morning. Craig seemed interested in this idea and they agreed that Craig would go to the home when he had dressed himself for three mornings. Craig and his parents sorted out his clothes each night when he went to bed. When they woke him in the morning they reminded him about dressing and if he was successful they praised him. Craig dressed himself for the next three days without any problem and had his trip to the animal home. He was keen to go again and his parents agreed that he could return after he had got dressed for four days. He was again successful and the programme went on for another two weeks. At the end of this time Craig and his parents agreed that they no longer needed a chart. He could visit the animal home each Saturday morning if he continued to dress himself.

Yasumi: time out for biting

Yasumi was three and had just started at playgroup. She was keen to go and enjoyed being with the other children, but she was not very good at sharing the toys. Yasumi would snatch toys from the other children and would bite if they refused to give them to her.

Yasumi's mother and the playgroup staff agreed that Yasumi needed to learn that biting was not acceptable. They decided to use time out and sent Yasumi to sit on a chair facing the corner of the room for two minutes whenever she bit another child. She was given a very simple instruction: 'Yasumi, we do not bite. Go and sit on the chair', and if she refused to go was firmly taken. After two minutes Yasumi was invited to come and play with the other children.

Yasumi refused to go to time out the first time she was sent and so was physically taken. She refused to sit down and kept trying to run away. The chair was facing the corner of the room so Yasumi's mother stood behind the chair. Every time Yasumi tried to stand up she gently but firmly put her hands on her daughter's shoulders and pushed her back on to the chair. She did not talk or argue with her and after about ten minutes Yasumi sat quietly in the chair. The next time she bit she refused to go to the time out chair but once taken sat quietly. After three weeks the biting had stopped.

DISCUSSION POINTS

1. What are the 'golden rules' of your house? Are you and your family clear what happens if they are broken?

2. Where could you use 'time out' in your house? What would you do if your child argued or refused to go?

3. What sort of rewards could you use to encourage your child to behave well?

3
Coping with Night-Time Problems

COMMON NIGHT-TIME PROBLEMS

The first few months following birth can be a very tiring time. Young babies do not have a regular sleep pattern and will wake and sleep whenever they want. Most will be waking two or three times each night, often to feed, and will be having short two- or three-hour blocks of sleep throughout the day.

By around six months of age babies begin to develop a more regular night-time routine and start to learn how to get themselves to sleep. They start to sleep through the night and the majority of sleep now takes place in one longer night-time block. Although most sleep occurs at night, many children will continue to have short daytime naps up until three or four years of age.

Most children learn good sleeping habits, but there are some who find it difficult to establish a regular night-time routine.

- About one in five pre-school children will be having some sort of night-time difficulty. Boys and girls are equally likely to develop night-time problems.

- Unfortunately children do not grow out of these difficulties. Babies with sleep problems are more likely to continue to have these difficulties when they reach school age.

For parents, night-time difficulties are hard to cope with. They have less time for themselves to relax. A large part of each evening is spent trying to settle a restless or unhappy child. Disrupted nights and a lack of sleep may make them feel tired and irritable and this may affect relationships with their partner, friends or relatives, or their performance at work.

There are four main types of night-time problems.

Settling difficulties
Some children become upset or refuse to settle when put to bed. At any

one time approximately one in twelve parents will have settling difficulties like these:

- crying, shouting or screaming when you put your child to bed

- insisting that you stay with them until they fall asleep

- repeatedly calling out once in bed

- refusing to stay in their own bed or bedroom

- refusing to go to bed when asked

- taking a long time to fall asleep.

Night-time waking
Frequent or regular night-time waking is very common. Of children aged one to two years of age:

- 56 per cent have been found to wake up to one night per week

- 24 per cent wake two to four nights per week

- 20 per cent wake five to seven nights per week.

By the age of three, around one in every six children will be regularly waking at night. Of these, some will be waking only once whereas others will be waking several times each night. On some occasions children will be waking for a feed but this should be unnecessary for children over about six months of age. They should be able to take the food they need during the day.

Refusing to sleep in their own bed
Some children will refuse to sleep in their own bed. A number of these will insist that they sleep in their parents' bed whereas others may end up falling asleep on the settee or whilst being held or rocked by their parent. Once settled, many parents will put the child in the child's own bed but they usually find that the child wants to come into their parents' bed or be held again if they wake up during the night.

About one in six parents of young children will find that their child will not fall asleep in their own bed.

Not getting enough sleep
Parents often worry that their children do not have enough sleep. They complain that their children are awake late at night or wake too early in the morning.

Children differ in the amount of sleep they need. This amount varies over time depending on the child's age but on average:

- during the first four weeks of life, babies will sleep an average of 16 hours per day

- by six to eighteen months, children will sleep for an average of 14 hours per day.

- by three years of age, the average amount of sleep goes down to 12 hours.

- at the age of five, it has reduced to about eleven hours each day.

COMMON CAUSES OF NIGHT-TIME PROBLEMS

Regular or persistent night-time problems are rarely due to any medical reasons. Understandably a short illness may cause some disruption to your child's night-time routine and they may become restless, wakeful and need extra reassurance and comfort. This should be a temporary phase and the sleeping pattern should return to normal once they are well.

A few children have enlarged tonsils or adenoids and these can obstruct their breathing, particularly at night. The breathing passage can become narrow making it harder to breathe which in turn may wake the child. The symptoms of this are:

- regular and very loud snoring at night

- difficulty breathing or catching their breath

- very restless sleeping

- frequent waking.

If you are concerned about his possibility, then talk with your family doctor.

The majority of sleeping difficulties are learning problems where the child has failed to develop a good night-time routine. There are five common reasons why this can happen.

1. Failing to learn how to fall asleep

Getting off to sleep is a skill that children have to learn. Parents with young babies often help their child by cuddling or rocking them. They may give them a bottle to suck whilst talking or singing in a quiet soothing voice. Many will hold their child until they are asleep and then put them into their cot. In these examples children will associate having a bottle and being held with going to sleep, events that are called 'sleep cues'. Unfortunately these particular sleep cues do not teach children how they can fall asleep on their own. If they wake during the night they will be unable to return to sleep without being picked up or fed by their parent.

As children get older they may insist that their parent stays with them until they fall asleep. Once again, if the child wakes during the night they will probably need their parent to sit with them until they return to sleep.

In both these examples the children have failed to learn how to fall asleep on their own.

2. No clear night-time routine

Young children have no concept of time and so do not know when to go to bed. They need their parents to tell them when it is time to sleep. A clear and predictable night-time routine is an important way of helping children learn when it is bedtime.

For many families everyday life is busy and some parents find it difficult to establish a regular and consistent routine. One day a child may, for example, be watching a video at eight o'clock whilst the next day they will be sent to bed at six o'clock. There may not be a settling routine which calms the child so they may go straight from playing a game of chase to being put to bed in a matter of minutes. At other times a child may go straight to bed and then constantly shout for a drink, something to eat, a story, light turned on, etc.

In these examples there is no clear and predictable night-time routine that calms the child and prepares them for sleep. The lack of a consistent settling routine creates unsettled children who are unready to sleep.

3. Learning that being awake is more fun

If given a choice, children will rarely take themselves to bed. Most will want to stay up and be with their family and join in with anything that might be going on. Watching television, listening to a story, sitting on a parent's lap, playing games, having a drink or simply talking are generally seen by most children to be better than going to sleep.

Some children learn that, although refusing to go to bed or waking at night may produce a few harsh words from their parent, it may also result in some benefits. They may be allowed to stay downstairs, to go into their parents' bed or to have a bottle of milk. For some children these benefits outweigh being told off and will increase the chance that they will behave this way again. These children have learned that refusing to go to sleep results in a number of benefits.

4. Worry or recent change

Children, like their parents, worry and become unsettled by change. All children feel worried or unsure at some time and for some this may affect their sleeping pattern. Their worries may make it difficult for them to get off to sleep or they may become more wakeful during the night. You may find that this occurs at certain times such as before a visit from their father or before playschool. A regular pattern like this would suggest that something is worrying your child.

Children also worry about their parents and notice if things are not quite right. Their refusal to go to bed may be their way of wanting to stay up to make sure that everything is alright. Coming into your bed may be their way of cheering you up or keeping you company, and over time this may become a learned habit.

5. Parental worry

Children need their parents to provide them with clear and predictable rules that are firmly and consistently applied. Typically children test these rules and sometimes become angry or upset as they learn that they are unable to do as they wish. This sort of confrontation can be difficult for parents who understandably do not want their children to be distressed and may lead them to worry and question whether they are doing the 'right thing'. Some parents become anxious and will give in to their child's demands letting them stay up, for example, or sleep in their bed rather than have a confrontation.

NIGHTMARES AND NIGHT TERRORS

Times of restless sleep in which children thrash about, talk and on some occasions sleep walk are quite common. These are partial wakenings that happen as a child moves from one stage of sleep to another. Perhaps the most difficult to understand and most worrying of these wakenings are nightmares and night terrors.

Nightmares and night terrors appear the same and are often wrongly confused by parents. Figure 7 shows the main differences between them.

	Nightmare	Night terror
When does it happen?	Usually in the early hours of the morning.	Often within the first 2/3 hours of going to bed.
What happens?	Child seems frightened. Often upset, crying, talking.	Appears terrified. Thrashing about, muttering, moaning.
How do they react to you?	Notices that you are there. Will answer your questions. May want comforting.	Seems unaware of you. Will not reply to your questions. May resist if you try and hold them.
Are they awake?	Wide awake.	May have eyes open but does not seem fully awake.
How quickly do they return to sleep?	May take a time to calm and settle.	Very quickly.
Do they remember anything the next day?	Can recall some parts of the dream.	No memory of anything at all.

Fig. 7. Nightmares or night terrors.

Dealing with nightmares

A nightmare is a scary dream which has woken the child. The child is awake and will talk with you and tell you something about what has happened. They will be frightened and will probably need calming and comforting before they are able to return to sleep. If your child has had a nightmare then:

- talk about it and find out what the nightmare was about

- find out what triggered it – story, television programme, etc.

- remember to avoid these 'triggers' before bedtime in the future

- reassure your child that the bad dream has gone.

Dealing with night terrors

A night terror is a partial wakening from a very deep stage of sleep. The child is still asleep and will not recognise you or reply to your questions and will remember nothing about it the next day. Night terrors tend to run in families and occur more often in boys and older children of 5–12 years of age. If your child has night terrors:

- Don't worry — these are fairly common and are not usually a sign of distress.

- Do not wake your child since this can scare them.

- Leave them alone, ensure that they are safe, and eventually they will return to sleep.

- Do not talk about it the next day. They will not remember anything about it.

ESTABLISHING A GOOD NIGHT-TIME ROUTINE

You can start to help your baby develop a good night-time pattern from about six months of age. This involves three key steps:

1. developing a regular bedtime routine

2. helping your baby distinguish between sleep and play time

3. leaving your baby to fall asleep on their own.

Developing a regular bedtime routine

The bedtime routine aims to calm your baby and prepare them for sleep. It is important that it is predictable and that events follow in the same order, such as:

    bath
    nightclothes
    upstairs to bedroom
    story/song
    feed
    put into cot
    kiss goodnight
    leave.

Try and make sure that the routine remains the same and that you put baby in their cot by the same time each night. There will be times when this routine will obviously vary, but in the early days try and stick with it as closely as you can.

Distinguishing between sleep and play time

An early task for parents is to teach their baby to distinguish between the time to sleep and the time to play. Baby needs to learn that sleeping takes place at night and that play and games take place during the day. Try and help your baby learn some sleep cues, events that they associate with going to sleep. These could include making the room darker, putting them in their cot, and giving them their 'night-time teddy'. If they are being fed during the night you could try and make daytime and night-time feeds different in the following way:

Night-time	Daytime
Keep lights dim	Light
Try not to over-stimulate baby	Make feeds interesting
Avoid playing with baby	Play games, sing
Keep quiet, little talking	Talk in normal voice
Put down as soon as finished feeding	Hold and cuddle as long as you like

Leaving baby to fall asleep on their own

Babies have to learn how to fall asleep on their own. In order to help your baby do this:

- Try and make sure that they sleep in the same place. This will help your baby learn that it is time for sleep when they go into their cot.

- Put baby in their cot for both daytime and night-time sleeps.

- Always put baby down awake. Wherever possible avoid rocking them to sleep and then placing them in their cot.

- Leave them with a soft toy to cuddle.

- Leave baby to get themself to sleep. They may not settle straight away and may cry for a few minutes.

Putting your baby down awake is important. They will fall asleep in the same place they awake and this will help them feel safe and secure about going to sleep.

DEALING WITH SETTLING PROBLEMS

There are different types of settling problems and each needs a slightly different approach. The first task is to clearly find out what is happening at night-time.

Keeping a diary

You may think that you already have a clear picture, but it is surprising how much more you can discover if you write it down. Often parents over- or underestimate the time things take. They are not always clear about what happens, whether certain nights are different, and whether some ways of dealing with things are more successful than others.

A useful way of getting things clear is by keeping a diary for about one or two weeks about what happens at bedtime. Your diary should include the day, time, what happened, what your child did, and what you did.

Figure 8 shows an extract from Mary and Peters' diary about their four-year-old son Carl's bedtime behaviour. The diary highlighted a number of things for Mary and Peter.

Day and time	What happened?	What did Carl do?
Weds, 7.30	Mary asked Carl to go to bed.	Ignored me, sat watching TV.
7.45	Told him to go up quickly, it was late.	Sat watching TV.
7.50	I said that he would have no sweets tomorrow unless he went to bed.	Carl cried, sat sobbing on the settee for 5 minutes. Then went upstairs.
8.00	Carl came down saying he couldn't find his pyjamas. Told him they were in his room.	Carl cried, saying they weren't there. I went and found them.
8.10	Carl came back down saying he was hungry.	Went and got him a drink. Carl sat on the settee with me to drink it.
8.25	Carl finished his drink. Told him it was bedtime and took him upstairs.	Carl came up with me and got into bed.

Fig. 8. Carl's bedtime diary

1. They did not have a calming bedtime routine that started to prepare Carl for sleep. Carl went from watching television to bed.

2. Mary and Peter did not always follow through their requests clearly or firmly. It was fifteen minutes from the first time Mary asked Carl to go to bed until she asked him again.

3. Mary and Peter were not involved in helping Carl get ready for bed. They asked him to go to bed rather than going with him and helping. When they eventually did take him Carl settled quickly.

Once Mary and Peter found out what was happening they decided to change how they dealt with bedtimes. They developed a bedtime routine which they firmly stuck with. They became more actively involved in helping Carl prepare for bed and started to read him stories in his room to calm him.

'My baby cries when I put her in her cot'

A number of parents find that their baby or child cries when they put them to bed. This often happens because their child has not learned to fall asleep on their own. In order to help your child, the first step is to make sure that there is a predictable calming night-time routine that prepares them for sleep. Secondly check that they have clear sleep cues which signal that it is time for sleep. These may include being put into their bed, cuddling a toy, being in a darkened room, a music tape playing gently, etc. The final stage is to leave them to cry themselves to sleep.

It is often this last stage that parents find most difficult since listening to a crying child is understandably distressing. Parents become worried and will often go and pick up their child to comfort them. There are no easy answers but if you are determined there are two choices, controlled crying and ignoring, and each has its advantages and disadvantages.

	Advantages	*Disadvantages*
● Controlled crying	More reassuring for parents.	Usually takes longer for child to stop crying.
	Provides an opportunity to check that your child is OK.	Hard to keep seeing and leaving an upset child. Greater chance that you give up.
● Ignoring	Often gets quicker results.	May be difficult for parent to do.
	Don't have to keep seeing a distressed child.	Initially your child may cry even more.

Controlled crying

With this approach you leave your child to cry for short periods of time before you go and check them. Decide in advance how long you will wait and then gradually lengthen the period of time between each check. You may choose to start off with three minutes, then five, then seven and so on until you are checking only every fifteen minutes.

The main purpose of checking is to reassure you that your child is OK so it is important that when you check your child you:

- do not pick them up

- avoid talking with them

- stay in the room for as short a time as possible.

You may find that your child will take a while to settle and it will probably take between four and seven nights before that fall asleep without crying. Stick with it and be firm.

Ignoring
With this approach you put your child to bed and leave them to cry themselves to sleep. This could take as long as an hour as your child learns that their crying no longer results in you coming.

Although this is difficult for some parents this approach often works very quickly and successful results are often achieved within four days. However, be warned that in the early days you may find that your child's crying becomes worse before they learn that you will no longer come. It is at this stage that you have to be firm and make sure that you do not give in. If you leave your child for thirty minutes and then give in, your child will cry for longer next time you try this method.

'We don't have a clear night-time routine'

Some children do not have a clear or predictable night-time routine which helps them calm and prepare for sleep. If bedtime varies too much then your children may well protest and refuse to go to bed on those days you send them to bed earlier.

In developing your routine:

- Make sure your routine is right for you and your family and fits in with your own evening timetable. If your partner does not return home until 7.00pm then they would be unable to spend time with their baby unless bedtime was later.

- Avoid chase or exciting games for at least thirty minutes before bedtime. Give your child a chance to calm down.

- Try and do things in the same order. Bath, pyjamas, up to bedroom, story, kiss goodnight, lights off. This will help your child learn the night-time routine.

- Think of any possible excuses for shouting and incorporate them into your night-time routine. Give your child something to eat and drink before they brush their teeth, glass of water by the bed, check that they have gone to the toilet, that they have their favourite teddy, etc.

● Make sure that they start the night in their own bed. Avoid your child falling asleep in one place, e.g. on the settee, and then being carried to their own bed.

'My child refuses to go to bed'

You can deal with the child who refuses to go to bed in two ways. You either adopt a firm approach and take them to their bed or you try and encourage them to go. Choose whichever method feels right for you.

The firm approach

Firmly but gently take them and give a clear message that it is now bedtime. Avoid arguments or drawn out discussions and do not chase them around the house since this may be seen by your child as a good game.

Some parents find this firm approach difficult since children may well become upset or angry at being made to go to bed. If you feel unable to carry it out and work through your child's resistance, it is better to try something else.

The encouraging approach

This approach tries to make going to bed more attractive by praising and rewarding the child for going to bed when you ask them. You can do this by using a behaviour chart (see Chapter 2).

Behaviour charts can be used for children of three years and older and are a simple but effective way of helping them learn that their good behaviour is noticed and praised.

Sara's behaviour chart

Jenny decided to use a reward chart to help her three-year-old daughter Sara go to bed when she was asked. Jenny told Sara that for every night she went to bed as soon as she was asked Sara could earn a special smiley face on her night-time chart. The chart was kept in Sara's bedroom and filled out as soon as she went to her room. If she earned a smiley face then Jenny made sure that Sara was praised and told how good she was. Sara loved stories and so Jenny made a point of reading a slightly longer bedtime story if she earned a smiley face as an extra treat. Sara's bedtime chart is shown in Figure 9.

Fig. 9. Sara's settling chart.

On Tuesday and Thursday of the first week Sara did not go to bed when she was asked. She did not earn a smiley face and did not have a bedtime story. Jenny did not make a big fuss about this but simply asked Sara to try and earn her smiley face tomorrow. For all the remaining days Sara earned her smiley faces, was praised and had her bedtime story.

'My child keeps coming out of his room or calls out'
On other occasions parents may find that their child will initially go to their room but will then keep coming out or calling for their parent. The two approaches we have already discussed can again be used at these times.

The firm approach
If your child comes out of their room for no good reason, it is important that they are quickly and firmly returned. You need to be firm, stay calm and give a clear message to your child that you are in charge:

● Do not get into long drawn out arguments about why they are not in bed.

● Ask them to go but if they refuse after the first request, take them.

● Avoid looking at them too much, keep calm and avoid smiling or laughing (which may signal to your child that you do not mean what you are doing).

● Repeat this every time they come out.

● If this happens many times each night, then sit outside their bedroom but never lock, bolt or tie their bedroom door shut. This is dangerous.

If your child keeps calling for you then make sure that your night-time routine covers all possible excuses for calling out. This will reassure you that they aren't really thirsty or hungry and have got a soft toy to cuddle, etc. The next stage is to ignore any of their shouts and so teach your child that their calls will not bring their parents. Ignoring is hard but it can be made easier to cope with:

● If you have a baby alarm then turn it off. Many parents sit listening for any sounds and the more you hear, the more you will want to go and check.

● Don't turn the sound down on the television. Carry on with what you want to do.

● If the shouting gets too much then don't sit listening to it. Go into the garden or to the back of the house and make a cup of tea.

● Arrange for someone to be with you to provide you with emotional support and help you stay firm. This could be your partner or a friend or relative.

The encouraging approach
Behaviour charts can be used to encourage children to be quiet or to stay in their room. Draw up a chart, explain to your child what you want them to do, and remind them when you tuck them in and kiss them good night. The chart will be filled out the next morning and if they have done as you asked remember to make a big fuss. If they have called or come out of their room, they will have an empty space on their chart. Remind them again the next night when you tuck them in and try again.

At other times your child may be coming out of their room or calling for you because they are unwell. This obviously needs a sympathetic approach and they will probably need more cuddles and reassurance at this time. However, once well, it is important that you again adopt a firm approach.

'My child takes a long time to go to sleep or wakes very early'

These sorts of problems are quite common, particularly in summer when the evenings and mornings are lighter. With these difficulties it is useful to start by keeping a diary to find out exactly how much sleep your child is having. Keep the diary for a week and write down when and for how long your child sleeps. Remember to include all sleep, including short naps in car seats or buggy and any sleep during the day. Once you have an idea of how much sleep your child is having the next stage is to try and make this happen in one block at night-time.

● If your child sleeps ten hours per day then they will not be able to go to bed at 7 o'clock each night and sleep through until 7 o'clock the next day. This is unrealistic so you will have to decide which you would prefer, earlier waking or a later bedtime.

● Some parents try and make their day busy and active in an attempt to tire their child out. This does not always work but it may be worth a try.

● If you want your child to sleep in the morning then push back the bedtime. Your child will be going to bed later but they will probably start to sleep longer in the morning. Stick with it for at least one week since your child's internal clock will need time to adjust.

● If you want your child to have an early bedtime then be prepared for early waking. You can make children go to bed but unfortunately you can't make them sleep. Thick lined curtains can sometimes help since they block out a lot of the daylight, make the room darker, and this may encourage your child to sleep

● Similarly, you cannot make children stay asleep, but you can encourage them to stay quietly in their room. Remember that young children are unable to tell the time and so when it is light they think that it is time to get up. You can help them learn when to get up by setting alarm clocks or lights on timer switches. If they awake early, then your child has to play quietly in their room until the alarm goes off or the light comes on.

'My child wants me to stay with him until he falls asleep'

Some children will only go to sleep if their parent stays and lies beside them. In this situation your child needs to learn that they can fall asleep on their own. You can help your child by a gentle gradual approach in which a series of small steps help your child learn to sleep on their own.

Peter was two and needed his mother to lay with him on his bed each night in order to go to sleep. This took approximately fifty minutes. Peter's mother decided to try the gradual approach and did the following:

Step 1:   Lay on Peter's bed but no longer cuddling him (2 nights)

Step 2:   Sit on Peter's bed, no cuddling (2 nights)

Step 3:   Sit on a chair besides Peter's bed (2 nights)

Step 4:   Sit on a chair in the doorway (2 nights)

Step 5:   Sit on a chair outside the door (3 nights)

In a few short steps Peter had learned that he no longer needed his mother to stay with him in order to sleep. The process was very gentle and was not distressing for either Peter or his mother.

In order to make this approach successful it is important that you:

• sit quietly and avoid talking with your child

• avoid playing any games

• ignore any of your child's questions

• try not to look at your child since this may encourage them to talk with you.

This will help your child learn that bedtime is a time for sleep and not another fun time.

'My child is afraid of her bedroom'

Some children will refuse to go to their own bedroom but will quite happily settle in their parents' bed or somewhere else. Occasionally this is because children are afraid or worried about being in their bedroom. They may have associated their bedroom with an unpleasant event (i.e. being left by their parent to go to sleep), experience (e.g. bad dream) or scary thought (e.g. monsters under the bed).

In this situation your child needs to learn that their bedroom is a nice, comfortable room and that there is no need to worry. You can do this in the following ways:

• Spend time with your child decorating the room and making it look pleasant. Rearrange the furniture, put up some pictures or perhaps redecorate or get a new bed cover. Involve your child so that they feel excited and positive about their new room.

• Talk about how nice their bedroom is so that your child keeps hearing a positive message which will counteract any of their doubts.

• Spend time playing in the room during the day. This gives your child a chance to be in their bedroom other than at night-time and so learn that there is nothing to be afraid of.

• Let your child have their light left on, a night light or the door left open if it makes them feel better.

• If they are worried about monsters then spend a minute or so each night 'chasing the monsters out'.

COPING WITH NIGHT-TIME WAKING

The other main type of night-time difficulties are waking problems. On some occasions you will find that your child wakes because they are in some discomfort, perhaps caused by wind or a wet or dirty nappy. You will probably know when this is the case and it is important that you go to them and sort these problems out. If their night-time waking happens more often or becomes more regular then it is likely that this has become a learned habit.

Night-time waking can take a number of different forms. Your child may wake and cry out for you, may get up and come into your bed, or may appear wide awake during the night but sleepy during the day. The first step is to try and find out more about such waking and your child's sleeping pattern.

Keeping a diary

A diary is a useful way of finding out how much sleep your child has, when they wake, and what happens once they do wake. The diary should record the day, time they sleep, time they wake up and what happens when they wake. Figure 10 shows an extract from the sleeping and waking diary of eighteen-month-old Mary. Mary's diary for the other six days was very similar and helped her parents see that:

Day	Time asleep	Time awake	What happened when awoke at night?
Monday	9.30am	11.20am	
	3.30pm	4.40pm	
	7.10pm	11.45pm	Gave a bottle of milk
	12.05am	2.50am	Rocked back to sleep
	3.00am	5.00am	Gave a bottle of milk
	5.30am	6.30am	Got up and played with her

Fig. 10. Mary's sleeping and waking diary

1. She slept about thirteen and a half hours each day, a fairly typical amount for a child of her age.

2. She was having three to four hours of this sleep during the day.

3. Whenever Mary woke at night her parents would go to her and
    would have to give her a bottle or a cuddle to get ger back to sleep.

Once Mary's parent became aware of this they tried to limit her daytime
sleep so that she slept more at night. When she did wake up they tried to
leave her to see if she could go back to sleep on her own.

'My child cries out during the night'

Night-time waking is common and many children stir or make noises
during the night. A number of these will successfully return to sleep
without disturbing their parents. If you hear a noise it is a good idea to
wait for a few minutes before you go and check. Parents sometimes react
too quickly and by going to your child too soon you may fully wake
them. Waiting a few minutes can give your child a chance to get themselves back to sleep again.

   Some children do not return to sleep and will fully awake and cry or
call out for their parents. At these times you have to teach your child that
they can return to sleep on their own by using the checking or ignoring
methods we have already discussed. This can be very difficult in the
middle of the night and will probably involve your child crying and
becoming distressed before they learn how to do this. It is important that
you plan very carefully how you will tackle this to make sure that you
will be successful:

●   Is it the right time to try and do this? If you are feeling very tired or
    someone in the family has an important meeting or exams coming
    up then it may be useful to wait. Choose a time when you are feel-
    ing stronger and when it doesn't matter quite so much if the fami-
    ly's sleep is disrupted.

●   Will you be able to stick with this plan for at least five days? If you
    are going away to visit friends at the weekend or on holiday then it
    will be better to wait until you return.

●   Prepare the neighbours and let them know what you are planning to
    do. Neighbours are often more understanding if you warn them in
    advance about possible night-time noise or disturbance.

●   If you have a partner then make sure that you both fully agree with
    this plan. You need to support and encourage each other to stick
    with it rather than disagree.

●   If you have other children tell them what you are going to do, apol-
    ogise for any inconvenience and offer them a special treat by way
    of compensation.

- Choose which method, checking or ignoring, you want to use.

- Decide what you will do if your child continues to cry and does not settle. Many parents lie in bed listening to the crying and this often makes things seem worse or more difficult. It may be better to go and make a cup of tea or get up and move further away so that you can hear less of the crying.

- Once you start it is very important that you stick with it and do not give in. If you feel unable to do this now then wait until you can. It is better not to try rather than to start and give up.

'My child comes into my bed'

Older children are able to get themselves up and some will come into their parents' bed during the night. For some families this is not a problem and they are quite happy with this arrangement, at least for the time being. Others would prefer that this does not happen and would like their children to sleep in their own bed throughout the night. If you decide that you would like to change things, the following ideas might be helpful:

- In order to teach your child to sleep in their own bed you need to ensure that they are firmly returned to their own bed every time they come into your room. If your child sneaks in whilst you are asleep then unfortunately there is little you can do about it.

- Firmly return your child to their own bed every time they come into your room. Persist with this to teach your child that they are no longer allowed to stay in your room.

- Do not get into arguments about this but quickly return your child to their own bed.

- Put a big 'no entry' sign on your bedroom door to act as a visual reminder to your child that they are not allowed in. In the morning you can change it to a big smiley face to show that they are now welcome.

- For younger children you can put a stair gate across their bedroom doorway to act as a barrier, but never lock or bolt children in their bedroom. This is dangerous and may make children become afraid of their bedroom.

- For older children you can use a behaviour chart to encourage them to stay in their own bedroom throughout the night.

Stopping night-time feeds

Most children do not need feeding during the night after about six months of age. If you are still giving your child night-time feeds then you can wean them off these in the following ways:

● If bottle feeding, the firm approach is to take the bottle and simply throw it away.

● A more gradual approach involves reducing feeds by a couple of ounces each night or reducing the number of feeds by substituting milk with water. Alternating milk with water is a possibility if you are breastfeeding. If you do this you may want to involve your partner in providing the water drink.

● To reassure you that your child is not hungry make sure that they have an opportunity to feed well before they go to sleep.

● Finally always remember to put your baby down awake.

HELPING YOUR CHILD TO SLEEP WELL

If you want to encourage your child to sleep well then think about the following twelve points.

1. Make sure that your child has a comfortable sleeping area in which they are put to bed each night.

2. Encourage them to play in their bedroom during the day to become familiar with their bedroom and learn that it is a safe place.

3. Check that the bedtime is OK and if your child takes a long time to settle think about making it later.

4. Make sure you have a clear calming night-time routine with fixed stages and a set bedtime. Avoid chase games before bed.

5. Minimise any excuses for shouting (drink, biscuit, etc.) and incorporate these into the night-time routine.

6. Always put your child into bed awake.

7. Leave doors open, lights on, music, mobiles, etc. if this helps your child to settle and sleep.

8. If they come out of their room, immediately and firmly return them to their bed.

9. If they shout or cry, try and ignore them.

10. If you have a partner, agree how you will deal with any night-time problems and how you will support each other.

11. Choose the right time to start your sleep programme.

12. Don't try anything unless you are determined and able to carry it through.

CASE STUDIES

Ishmael keeps coming out of his bedroom

Ishmael was four and had never slept very well. He had a very clear calming night-time routine and would be upstairs in bed at 7.30pm each night. He would not, however, settle and would be up and down the stairs about five or six times with excuse after excuse. Each time his parents gave him what he wanted and would send him back to bed until they eventually gave up. He would then sit with them to watch television finally falling asleep by about 9.00pm when he would be carried upstairs to his bedroom. He then stayed in his bed and slept until the morning.

Ishmael's parents were clear that they wanted to change this and would like Ishmael to stay in his own bedroom after they kissed him goodnight. They decided to start a programme and sat down with Ishmael and drew up a chart in which he coloured in a dinosaur every time he stayed in his bedroom when he went to bed. Once Ishmael earned three dinosaurs he would have a special treat of going on a picnic. If he earned another four he would go swimming.

Ishamael's parents talked about how they would deal with him if he did come out of his bedroom. They agreed that they would take him back to his room, quickly and firmly, as soon as he came out. They knew that there was no reason for him to come downstairs and so decided to ignore his requests. Ishmael's mother felt that she was the firmer of the parents and found this easier and so took the lead in this part of the programme.

For the first two days Ishmael was very good and stayed in his bedroom when he went to bed. On the third night he came downstairs seven or eight times but was firmly returned by his parents on every occasion. The same thing happened the following night and on the fifth day Ishmael's mother decided to sit outside Ishmael's bedroom. She took a book to read and sat on a chair outside his door. She completely ignored any of his talking and Ishmael stayed in his bedroom. The same thing happened the following three nights, and Ishmael became quieter and seemed to fall asleep more quickly. Ishmael's mother decided that she did not need to sit outside his room any more and Ishmael continued to fall asleep in his own bedroom without coming downstairs.

Jane takes a long time to fall asleep

Jane was three and lived in a ground-floor flat with her mother, Emma. Each night Emma would go through the same night-time routine and would kiss Jane goodnight at 6.00pm. Jane stayed in her bedroom, did not call out but was rarely asleep before 7.30pm. If Emma went to check she would find Jane playing quietly with her toys or looking at a book. In the morning she would often wake at about 7.00am.

Emma was worried that Jane was not sleeping enough and decided to keep a sleeping and waking diary for a week. The diary showed that Jane had no daytime naps and on average was sleeping almost twelve hours each day. This proved that Jane was having enough sleep and so Emma decided to let her daughter stay up later and put her to bed at 7.00pm. This seemed to do the trick and within half an hour of going to bed Jane was asleep.

Tom cries when put in his cot

Tom was eight months old and had never slept very well. His mother Mary always put Tom down in his cot awake but Tom would cry and become unhappy. After about five minutes Mary would pick him up and cuddle and rock him to sleep. The same things happened during the night and Mary became very tired and decided that things had to change.

Mary decided that she had to teach Tom to fall asleep on his own. He was always put down in his cot but this could be in the front room, or bedroom or hallway. Sometimes the room was dark and at other times it was light, sometimes noisy whilst at other times quiet. Mary decided to help Tom learn that certain things were associated with sleeping, i.e. sleep cues. She put him in his cot, in her bedroom with the curtains shut. Mary bought a special teddy which Tom only had at night-time. Finally Mary made sure that after she kissed him goodnight she left a musical mobile for Tom to watch.

The first time Tom was put down he was quiet for the first ten minutes, being fascinated by his new musical mobile. He then started to cry but Mary decided that she would try the gradual approach and left him for five minutes before she went and checked on him. When Mary went in she tucked Tom up, and wound up the musical mobile again. She did not pick him up or talk with him and was in and out of the room in less than a minute. Tom continued to cry, and every five minutes Mary would repeat this procedure until Tom fell asleep. She persisted with this routine and after three days Tom was happy to go into his cot and was able to get off to sleep on his own.

DISCUSSION POINTS

1. How can you help your baby learn when it is time to go to sleep and when it is time to be wakeful and play? What sleep cues can you use?

2. What can you do that will help you cope with your crying child and help you stay firm and not give in? Make a list of all your ideas, and begin to try them out. Which ones do you find most helpful, and why?

3. Write down your child's night-time routine. Are the steps clear, is the process calming, and do you and others always stick with it?

4
Encouraging Good Eating

COMMON EATING PROBLEMS

One of the most difficult challenges parents face is how to encourage
their children to eat an adequate amount and a good range of food. This
is seen by many as one of the basic tasks of being a good parent along-
side providing their child with love and protecting them from danger. In
view of the importance placed upon food it is not surprising that for
many parents eating and feeding becomes a stressful and emotive event.

Eating problems are common in pre-school children:

- About one in six pre-school children will have some form of eating
  difficulty. At this age there is no difference between boys and girls
  in the rates of eating problems.

- These difficulties last over time. It has been found that two-thirds of
  children who have an eating problem at the age of three continue to
  have difficulties at the age of four. One-third will continue to have
  problems at the age of eight.

- By the age of five, one in three parents will describe their child as
  having a mild or moderate eating problem.

- Eating problems are more common in children of low birth weight.

There are three main types of feeding and eating problems:

1. poor appetite

2. faddy eating

3. poor mealtime behaviour

Poor appetite
Some children seem totally disinterested in food. They appear indiffer-
ent to eating or will take a long time to eat tiny amounts.

● About one in five three-year-old children are described by their parents as having a poor appetite.

Whilst many parents feel that their children do not eat enough, most will continue to grow and appear healthy. Parents often expect their children to eat more than they actually require. In many situations the belief that a child is not having enough to eat is due to unrealistic parental expectations. If your child is healthy, has energy and continues to grow then they are probably eating as much as they need.

Faddy eating

Many parents complain that their child's diet is very limited consisting of only a few different foods.

● Between one in ten and one in six pre-school children are extremely faddy with their eating.

This may be because they will only eat a few preferred foods, refuse to try anything new, only eat soft-textured or puréed food, or prefer drinking milk to eating. At other times children may eat but will prefer things that their parents consider to be 'junk food'.

Poor mealtime behaviour

Some children will have a good appetite and will eat a wide range of different foods. For their parents problems can sometimes arise because of how they behave during mealtimes. This can take many different forms and may include:

● constantly climbing out of their seat

● spitting out food

● using fingers to eat instead of a spoon and fork

● messy eating or playing with food

● walking around the house eating rather than sitting at the table

● refusing to feed themselves

● retching or making themselves sick.

COMMON CAUSES OF EATING PROBLEMS

In a few cases children may lose weight or fail to grow at the expected rate. A temporary weight loss may be nothing to be concerned about and is common particularly after illness. Similarly some children are born small and will continue to be small although they grow at the correct rate for their size. If, however, a weight loss persists over time, or your child grows at a slower or faster rate than expected, then it would be useful to discuss this with your family doctor. About one or two children in every hundred have severe problems with their speed of growth which require careful monitoring by your health visitor, family doctor or a paediatrician.

Working out the expected growth of a child needs to be done by a health professional. Your family doctor or health visitor will be able to do this by using growth charts. These are made by plotting the height and weight of a large number of children over time. Comparing your child with these helps to see whether your child is growing at the right speed.

The majority of eating problems are not, however, due to any medical reason. Most problems are caused by children failing to learn how to eat properly for one or more of the following reasons.

Food or mealtimes become associated with unpleasant feelings

Eating or mealtimes can become an unpleasant experience for some children. As they learn to bite, chew and cope with different textured foods they may sometimes gag, retch or vomit. Food eaten at a later date may remind them of these feelings and may make them see food as something unpleasant which they try to avoid by refusing to eat.

At other times mealtimes may become very stressful. Children may be threatened, coaxed, force fed or made to sit at the table for hours until they have eaten their food. In these situations children may learn that mealtimes are unpleasant events which they try to avoid by refusing to eat or refusing to come to the table.

Finally, eating can be a sociable activity but many children find themselves eating on their own. Parents may not eat with their children, or eat different foods resulting in children failing to learn that food is fun and enjoyable. For many children starting school is the answer to their eating problems. Finding themselves with others who are eating and trying a range of different foods is often enough to stimulate their interest and show them that food can be enjoyed.

Children have not learned to try different foods

Young children are totally dependent upon their parents to prepare and provide them with a range of different foods. If a parent only gives their child milk then the child will only learn to eat and cope with liquid foods and will probably reject anything new or different.

Eating problems can arise because children have not learned to try different textured foods. As a baby they may have preferred milk, or been unable to cope with lumpy or textured food and so continue to be fed liquid or finally puréed meals. Anything more solid will probably be rejected resulting in concerned parents feeding the child what they want as they try to make sure that their child eats.

Similarly there is nothing more frustrating than spending time preparing a meal, only to find that your child refuses to eat it. This makes parents give up and resort to feeding their child what they know they like. By doing this the parent is unknowingly encouraging their child to eat a more limited and restrictive diet.

Children learn that refusing to eat gets them noticed

Children who refuse to eat often receive considerable attention as their parents try to encourage and cajole them to eat. This is often in contrast to those children who eat well. They are usually left to get on with their food and receive little or limited attention or positive praise from their parents. Most children like adult attention even if it is critical or telling them off, and a number learn that refusing to eat is a good way of getting it.

Observations of parents at mealtimes has shown that parents try many different things to get their children to eat. Some try to encourage their children to eat, bribing them or offering wonderful incentives in exchange for eating a few mouthfuls of food. Various games are tried as parents feed their children or follow them around trying to force spoonfuls of food into their mouths. Preferred foods are prepared one after another in the hope that the child may eventually eat something.

Other parents become more critical and will constantly talk about how little their child has eaten. In all these situations children learn that refusing to eat results in considerable parental attention.

ENCOURAGING CHILDREN TO EAT WELL

The child's ability to feed and cope with a wider range of different textured and flavoured foods grows over time.

● Babies are born with the ability to suck and can feed straight away from the breast or bottle.

● Initially they have a preference for sweet tastes as found in milk.

● By about four months of age babies have gained better control of their tongues and are now able to use this to guide food around their mouths.

● This is the time parents should start to introduce baby or puréed foods into their children's diet.

● Babies will also start to express a preference for more savoury foods.

● By approximately six months babies will hold on to a bottle or cup and as they get their teeth they will start to bite and chew.

● By twelve months they can cope with firmer textured foods that require more chewing and will start to finger feed foods such as bread, biscuits and toast fingers.

● By about eighteen months many children are able to drink from a beaker, and can use a spoon to feed.

● Using a knife and fork starts to occur by between two and three years of age.

In order to encourage children to progress down this pathway parents have to:

● wean their children off milk

● introduce more textured foods into their diet

● provide their children with a range of foods and flavours

● encourage them to feed themselves.

Weaning

The age that parents wean their children varies and there are no hard and fast rules which say that this must be done by a particular age. This is largely up to the parent and what feels comfortable for them. Some parents enjoy breastfeeding, worry that their child may feel rejected if this is stopped, and will continue to feed for a number of years. Others find this to be very restrictive and will be keen to completely phase out liquid feeds after the first year. Whenever you choose to do this the chances of success will undoubtedly be increased if you feel sure and committed to your decision.

Weaning can be made easier if it is done in gradual stages:

● Decide how many feeds you will give your baby each day. This moves towards a more structured feeding approach instead of feeding on demand.

● You may want to phase out certain feeds. Some parents feel more comfortable starting with the daytime feeds whereas others are keen to eliminate the night-time ones.

- Start to offer your child milk after they have eaten some solid food.

- Offer your child drinks in trainer beakers.

- Introduce some puréed baby foods by three to four months of age.

- To start with, give very small amounts (i.e. teaspoonfuls) and gradually increase the amount over time.

- Provide a wide range of different flavoured and textured food.

- Encourage finger foods.

Making food and mealtimes enjoyable

One of the key lessons a child needs to learn is that food is enjoyable and mealtimes are fun. Stressful mealtimes or unpleasant food experiences may make a child reluctant to eat.

- Try and make sure that mealtimes are a sociable occasion. Try and eat at least some meals together and show your child how to eat.

- Even if you are not eating, sit down with your child whilst they eat. Sitting on their own is unattractive to children who will be more interested in what you are doing rather than eating their food.

- Try and eat meals at the same place. This will help your child learn that when they sit at the table they eat.

- Try and make mealtimes regular.

- Make mealtimes fun for children. Avoid talking about how little they have eaten and above all avoid force feeding or threatening.

- Relax and try to enjoy it.

Providing a varied diet

Young children have little choice about what food they eat. Parents choose and prepare the food. It is therefore important that you provide your child with a wide-ranging and varied diet.

- Provide different flavoured and textured foods.

- If they do not eat one food during a meal then don't give up straight away. Try it again on another occasion.

- Avoid feeding only those foods you know your child likes. This can start to restrict their diet and make them reluctant to try different foods.

- Be prepared to compromise. Not all 'junk' food is bad and if this is what your child likes, be prepared to offer them this for a fixed number of meals each week.

- Presentation is important. Try to make the food look appealing and this will encourage your child to try it.

- Give older children a choice about some of the meals they eat. Limit the choice to either this or that. If you give more than two options or leave it very open children may find it difficult to make up their minds.

COPING WITH FADDY EATING

Some parents feel that their child is extremely faddy and will only eat a very few foods. This results in meals becoming repetitive and parents feeling frustrated and concerned about their child's diet.

What does your child eat?

If you are worried about what your child eats, a useful first stage is to make a list of all the things they eat and have eaten. Think about everything they have ever eaten even if it has only been once or twice. Check with others who may care for your child such as nursery staff, childminder, relatives or friends. You may find that your child will eat more foods than you realised.

Jamal's eating list

Jamal was eighteen months old and his parents felt that he would eat very little other than bread, toast, crisps, cheese, baked beans and biscuits. They decided that they would make a list of all the foods Jamal now eats, what he had eaten, and what he would eat when he went to Lyn, the childminder. The list is shown in Figure 11.

Foods Jamal eats at home	Food he has eaten in the past	Foods he will eat at Lyn's
Bread	Soup	Fish fingers
Toast	Fish fingers	Sausages
Crisps	Carrot	Spaghetti hoops
Cream crackers	Apple	Boiled egg
Baked beans	Sausage	Sandwiches – jam
Biscuits	Marmite	Grapes
Cheese	Pasta	Crisps
		Biscuits (all sorts)
		Cake (sponge cake)
		Apple (cut up)
		Raisins

Fig. 11. Foods Jamal eats

The list was quite a surprise for Jamal's parents and helped them realise that he would eat a wider range of foods than they had imagined. They had limited the range of foods they gave him wrongly believing that he would only eat certain things. The list was used to plan a varied menu of meals for a two-week period and much to his parents delight, Jamal ate most of what was provided.

'My child will only eat a few foods'

On other occasions food lists will confirm that your child is very faddy and will only eat a few foods. Most children go through a stage of faddiness in which they suddenly stop eating foods they previously liked. However, some children become extremely faddy and this can last a long time. Food faddiness can take different forms ranging from the child who will eat only a few things to those who will only eat a certain sort of chip or pizza or a food cooked in a particular way.

At these times there is a tendency for parents to prepare and present only those foods they know their children will eat. By doing this, parents are unknowingly encouraging their children to have a restricted diet. On these occasions the key task is to widen the range of foods that the children have access to. In order to do this parents can use either a firm or an encouraging approach.

The firm approach

If you ask a faddy eater what they would like to eat then inevitably they will come up with the same foods day after day. With the firm approach you decide what your child will have to eat and you present them with it. In doing this:

● Choose new foods that you suspect they will like. There will be some foods which your child will prefer to others. Choosing the more favoured foods will increase the chance that meals are eaten.

● Present the food with the expectation that it will be eaten.

● If your child refuses to eat it or has a temper, ignore them. Leave the food on the table.

● If they try the food, praise them, even if it is a tiny amount.

● Do not suggest or offer an alternative to the meal you have provided.

● After a fixed time (10-15 minutes), if the meal has not been eaten, take the plate away.

● Mealtime is now over. Avoid talking about how little they have eaten.

● If your aim is to encourage your child to try different foods, do not provide them with favoured snacks in between meals.

The firm approach can be difficult particularly if you are worried about your child's weight. If they refuse to eat, you may be tempted to give in and provide them with things you know they will eat. As an alternative, you could try being firm for only one meal per day, possibly the midday meal. Your child would continue to have their usual breakfast and tea which will reassure you that they do not start the day or go to bed hungry. If they refuse to eat the midday meal then they can still eat at tea and go to bed with a full stomach.

The gradual approach
A gentler approach is to continue feeding your child the foods they enjoy whilst making sure that you present them with a new food as well. If a child will eat, for example, sausages and chips, then prepare this but put a few baked beans on the plate as well. Similarly if they will eat a cheese sandwich, given them half a cheese sandwich as well as a new food, e.g. half an apple.

● Choose or discuss with your child those new foods that seem the most preferable.

● Present a small amount of the new food and the meal.

● Praise the child for eating or trying the new food.

● If they eat it then make sure that you incorporate it into their diet.

'My child will not try anything new'
Some children will refuse to try even a tiny amount of anything different. They will instantly dismiss it as horrible. The task at these times is to encourage the child to at least try the food.

● Decide on how many new foods you would like your child to try each week and plan when you will present them.

● Initially introduce those foods that you think your child will be more likely to enjoy. Early success will encourage you and your child to continue.

● Put a very small quantity on the plate (six or seven peas).

● Ask them to try the food.

- If they do, praise them.

- You can use a behaviour chart to emphasise this so that they earn a sticker for trying the new food.

- Do not expect them to eat all the new food. The important thing is that they have tried it.

- If they refuse to try it, ignore them and do not get into an argument.

- Repeat the request on two further occasions throughout the course of the meal.

- At the end of the meal take the plate away and if they have not tried it, they will not earn a sticker on their behaviour chart.

- Try again tomorrow.

HELPING YOUR CHILD TO EAT A REASONABLE AMOUNT

The second main concern is about the amount of food a child eats. Parents often feel that their children appear disinterested in food, do not eat enough or need lots of encouragement to eat. Others find that their children eat very slowly resulting in tiny amounts of food being eaten during the course of a meal.

There is no fixed amount of food that children need to eat at various ages. Parents make judgments about whether their children eat more or less than other children. Sometimes parents expect their children to eat more food than they actually require.

Keeping a food diary

If you are concerned about the amount of food your child eats, the first stage is to keep a diary of all the food and drink your child has over a one-week period. Write down the day, time and what they ate, as in the diary shown in Figure 12. The diary will help you see when, how much and what sort of things your child is eating or drinking.

Day and time	What did they eat or drink?
Monday	
7.30	large glass of milk
9.15	small bowl of cornflakes, half slice of toast and jam
11.00	2 biscuits and a glass of milk
12.10	packet of crisps and a milkshake
2.25	1 biscuit, half an apple, glass of squash
4.45	2 fish fingers, few chips, yoghurt, milkshake
5.30	glass of milk, chocolate bar

Fig. 12. Food and drink diary

'My child eats very little'

A few children eat very little and appear disinterested in food. If your child is healthy, full of energy and continuing to grow, there should be little to worry about. If you are concerned, talk about this with your family doctor or health visitor.

Children can be helped to become more interested in food by:

● Encouraging them to become involved in the preparation of food. This can be done in lots of ways such as helping you to bake a cake, arranging food on a grill pan, sprinkling grated cheese over a pizza or mixing ingredients together in a bowl. They will probably be more interested in trying the things if they have helped prepare them.

● Making sure that there are few distractions during mealtime. Turn the television and radio off and sit down with them at the table.

● Making the food look attractive and appetising. We tend to eat with 'our eyes' first and if it looks good then we will usually be more interested in trying it.

● Combining special treats with food, e.g. a trip to a hamburger restaurant or a picnic in the park.

Children can be helped to increase the amount of food they eat in the following ways:

● Start off by serving small portions of food on large plates. Large meals may seem overwhelming and it is helpful for children to learn that they can finish the food on their plate. The amount can be slowly increased over time.

● Make meals a sociable event. Inviting other children to tea can show your child that others enjoy and eat their food. This can motivate them to eat more.

● Increase your child's motivation to eat by using a behaviour chart or reward programme. Give them a sticker for eating their meal and make sure that you give them lots of praise for eating.

● Ignore them if they do not eat. Turn your attention to someone else who is eating.

● Keep calm and avoid talking about how little they have eaten.

● Have a fixed time for how long the meal lasts and clear the plates away at the end of this regardless of how much is eaten.

'My child eats lots of snacks'

A number of parents complain that their child will eat snacks through-out the day but will not sit down and eat a proper meal. Whilst this is frustrating the way you handle it depends upon what you want to achieve.

If you are concerned about your child's weight your overall task will probably be to get your child to eat more. Refusing to give your child food when they ask for it does not make sense. If this is the case:

● Give them snacks or food if they request it.

● Refusing can teach them that they can go longer without eating. In turn this may reduce their appetite and make them feel less hungry when they eventually do sit down to eat their meal.

● The golden rule is to feed small amounts often.

If you are not concerned about your child's weight but you want them to eat their meals or to eat different foods:

● cut out snacks

● limit how much milk they have

● if really hungry, provide alternative snacks such as raisins, carrots or apple segments.

'My child prefers drinks'

Some children will drink lots of milk or juice and will then be too full to eat their meal. These children are filling themselves up with too much liquid. To get them to eat you need to get them to drink less.

The first stage would be to record how much they are drinking each day. If it appears a lot or if they have drinks before their meals then try reducing them:

● Cut down the number of drinks they have particularly those just before meals

● Buy a special cup which is smaller than their current one. To your child they will still be having their cupful of drink but the cup is now smaller.

● Half fill bottles or cups. Often children will drink what they are given irrespective of whether they really need it.

● If they ask for a drink just before a meal then ask them to wait. If they are unable to, then provide them with a very small drink.

'My child eats too much'

There is a tendency for present-day children to become more over-weight. Less physical exercise, a more sedentary lifestyle and a better diet are obvious reasons. Once the weight has been put on it is hard for it to come off.

Putting young children on diets is not a good idea and should not be done unless it is carefully monitored by a dietician or child care professional. Calorie-controlled diets are rarely required but there are some things you can do to help your child lose weight.

● Avoid too many sweets, sugary foods.

● Provide low fat alternatives wherever possible, e.g. low fat spread, cheese, etc.

● Fill your child up with carbohydrates such as bread, potatoes and pasta.

● Limit snacks between meals.

● If your child persists provide a low fat alternative such as sticks of carrot, celery or apple.

● Try to get your child to do more everyday exercise. Walk to the shops or park instead of going in the car.

● Involve your child in more active pastimes — gym club, dancing, etc.

IMPROVING MEALTIME BEHAVIOUR

The last group of common eating concerns are about the way children behave at mealtimes. Some children refuse to sit down, throw food, eat with their fingers or are generally unpleasant to sit with during a meal.

Children younger than three

One of the most important ways you can help younger children to eat better is to make sure that their poor mealtime behaviour results in little attention. Often children who mess with their food get a lot of adult attention. Children like attention even if you are telling them off and this may encourage them to behave this way again in the future.

● Make sure they get your attention for eating well.

● Ignore minor misbehaviour or silliness.

● For more extreme behaviour remove your child from the table for a couple of minutes and then try again. Repeat this process as many times as you need to.

● Set a limit to the length of each meal. If food has not been eaten at the end of this time then remove it. Mealtime is now over.

Children over three years of age

The best approach to these sorts of problems for children of this age is to set up a behaviour chart.

● Agree how you would like your child to behave during mealtimes and try to define this positively. This means telling your child what you would like them to do rather than what you would like them to stop doing. Tell them to 'sit at the table' rather than 'stop wandering about'; 'eat with your knife and fork' rather than 'stop eating with your fingers'.

● Once agreed tell your child how you expect them to behave and introduce your behaviour chart. Making the chart look exciting and special will increase your child's interest.

● Before you start each meal remind your child about the chart and about how you expect them to behave.

● If they are successful, praise them at the end of the meal and award a sticker.

● If they are unsuccessful, ignore them as much as you can and they will not earn a sticker on their chart.

● Try to get other people who visit the house to look at the chart but remember to make sure that they talk about those times that your child has eaten and behaved well.

HELPING YOUR CHILD TO EAT WELL

The following twelve points will help your child develop a good eating pattern.

1. Make mealtimes pleasant and try and remove the stress/focus on eating.
2. Make mealtimes sociable. Involve other children and adults to demonstrate that eating is fun and mealtimes are enjoyable.
3. Make food look appetising and attractive. Involve your children in the preparation of meals.
4. Serve small portions and offer food frequently throughout the day.
5. Provide your children with a range of foods of different textures.
6. Provide your children with some of their favourite foods but at other times present them with new foods to try.

7. Having meals in a set place helps children learn that it is time to eat.

8. Allow a fixed time for the duration of the meal. If the meal is not eaten at the end of this time then take food away with no comment.

9. Avoid force feeding, coaxing or threatening. Do not talk about how little has been eaten or how difficult children have been to feed in front of them. Try and reduce the amount of attention they receive for not eating.

10. Give your children attention when eating or attending to food and praise them if they have eaten well.

11. Try to combine special occasions with eating, e.g. going for a picnic, a visit to MacDonalds.

12. Once your children have tried a new food, incorporate and integrate it into their diet.

CASE STUDIES

Billy is a faddy eater

Billy was four and his parents were worried about his diet. He would eat so few foods that it prevented Billy from going to birthday parties or his friend's house for tea. His parents were cross that they had to make him different food from the other children and frustrated about the range of meals they could prepare him.

They kept an eating list for a week which showed that Billy would only eat pasta and would not eat rice, potatoes or bread. His parents felt that mealtimes would become less stressful and Billy's life less restricted if he would eat at least two of these foods.

Billy's parents sat down with him and went through lots of different foods which they sorted into three piles. The first was those foods that Billy thought would be really bad and which he would not even think about trying. The second pile consisted of foods that he thought might be OK but he was not keen to try. The last pile was foods he thought were OK and those he would be most prepared to try. This pile included bread and rice.

A reward programme was introduced where Billy coloured in a section of a lighthouse whenever he tried a new food. It was agreed that he would try a small portion of at least two new foods a week from the pile he was most prepared to taste. His parents agreed that once he had tried six new foods, they would take him to the seaside for the day.

Billy tried two new foods in the first week including rice which was not as bad as he thought. He tried a further two foods the next week and three new things the week after, and the family went to the seaside as agreed. This plan continued and the number of foods he would eat slowly increased. The new foods he thought were alright were incorporated into his diet and presented again in slightly larger portions. After two months Billy was eating rice and bread, mealtimes were less stressful and he was having similar meals to the rest of the family.

Sam will not sit at the table

Sam was two and a half and would not stay in his seat during mealtimes. He would climb down and run around the house although he would occasionally come back to the table to pick up pieces of food. Quite often one or other of his parents would go after him and would walk around the house trying to feed him. Mealtimes had become a game of chase for Sam and he was receiving considerable attention from his parents who were running around the house after him.

Sam's parents decided that things had to change. They agreed that as a family they would eat their meals together giving them an opportunity to show Sam how to behave at the table. If Sam wanted anything to eat he would now have to sit at the table. If he got out of his seat they would ignore him and not run after him. They would not give him any food unless he was sitting at the table and if he did eat they would praise him up. At the end of the meal any uneaten food was removed and Sam was not given anything else to eat until the next meal.

For the first few meals Sam continued to behave badly. He kept coming up to his parents who were sitting at the table. They ignored Sam so he started to throw his food around. This was very calmly dealt with by his father who simply removed his meal and for the first day Sam ate very little. He was hungry at breakfast the next day and was ready to sit and eat at the table. He did wander off a couple of times but his parents remained seated and did not follow him around with food. By the end of the first week Sam's mealtime behaviour had greatly improved and he was now sitting for longer at the table. He still occasionally wandered off but he had now learned that eating only happens at the table.

Mandy will not give up her bottle

Mandy was fifteen months old and would drink milk from her bottle all day long. She would eat solid foods but she preferred to drink and would be full of milk by mealtime so that she ate very little.

Mandy's mother decided to reduce the amount of milk Mandy drank. She decided that she would only give her a bottle at night-time and that during the day she would have small amounts of weak juice. Mandy accepted this very well and there were only a few times when she demanded her bottle. Her mother remained firm, did not give in, and Mandy started to eat more solids and drink less milk.

DISCUSSION POINTS

1. How many ways can you think of to encourage your child to eat a varied diet?

2. How can you change your mealtimes to make them more enjoyable?

3. What can you do to stay calm at mealtimes and to help you praise your child for eating?

5
Dealing with Toileting Problems

COMMON TOILETING PROBLEMS

Toilet training starts for many children around the age of two. Nappies are removed during the daytime and children are introduced to the idea and encouraged to use the potty. Some children take to this very quickly and soon become dry and clean. Others seem to take longer and will continue to poo or wet their nappy or pants.

Problems with toileting are quite common in pre-school children.

Daytime wetting

● One in four three-year-old children wet themselves during the day at least once a week.

● Daytime wetting is much more common in girls.

Night-time wetting

● Half of all three-year-old children and one in seven five-year-old children wet the bed at least once per week.

● Night-time wetting is more common in boys.

● First-born children tend to be slower to become dry at night.

● Often children who wet at night have a parent who suffered in a similar way.

Soiling

● At the age of three between one in ten and one in six children will be messing their pants at least once per week.

● By the age of five most children have become clean and only three in every hundred will be messing themselves.

● Boys are two to four times more likely to soil than girls.

COMMON CAUSES OF TOILETING PROBLEMS

Medical reasons

Medical causes of **wetting** are unusual with perhaps the most common being urinary tract infections. The main symptom is discomfort during urination, often described as a tingling or burning sensation. Some children seem more prone than others to these infections, but they can be quickly and easily treated by your doctor.

Similarly, medical causes for **soiling** are rare although a number of children do suffer from constipation. This can make pooing very difficult and may require the child to sit on the toilet and push for some time until they are successful. These children may poo very infrequently or pass very large poos which they find painful. For many, pooing becomes associated with pain and so they try and hold on to their poo to try and avoid any future discomfort. This makes the problem worse and creates the constipation cycle shown in Figure 13.

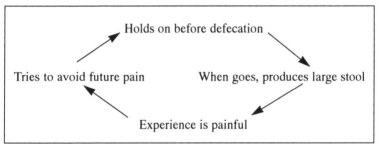

Fig. 13. The constipation cycle

Some children become very badly constipated and will need the help of the family doctor or paediatrician. Signs of constipation may include:

● Infrequent passage of poos.

● Your child may have extended tummy or look 'pot bellied'.

● Small, hard, pelleted poos.

● A foul smelling liquid that looks like diarrhoea. This overflow soiling is caused by faeces liquifying and seeping out around the constipated mass in the child's bowel. The hard, compacted faeces that cause constipation need to be removed. This can be done by using medicines which soften the faeces and stimulate the bowel to empty. Your family doctor should be able to help.

'Tuning in' takes time

Toilet training is a complicated process. Children have to:

- tune into and understand the feelings in their bowels and bladder that tell them it is time to go to the toilet

- learn that they do their poos and wees in the toilet

- learn how to wait and hold on until they get to the right place

- teach themselves how to start and stop pooing and weeing

- learn how to clean themselves up afterwards.

This process of 'tuning in' takes time and some children take longer than others. It is reassuring to know that most children do get there eventually.

- The majority of children are clean and dry during the day by the age of five.

- Most children will have become dry at night by the age of seven.

Emotional upset
Toileting accidents are sometimes a sign that your child is unhappy or worried. This is more likely to be the case if your child has been dry or clean for a number of weeks and then starts to have accidents. These may be occasional accidents which last for just a few weeks or they happen every day and seem to go on for months.

Try and think about what else was happening at the time the accidents started. For example, did they start closely after the birth of a new baby or when they started at playgroup? You may also find that accidents only happen on certain days or when certain people are around. If this is the case, your child may be trying to tell you that they are worried about something.

Failed to learn what to do
For children who have never been dry or clean, the problem may be that they have not yet learned what to do. They may not have been taught to sit on the potty or the toilet to wee and poo. These children learn that these things are done in their nappy. Others may not have learned how to defecate and may sit on the toilet and expect something to happen without really trying.

Another group of children learn that going to the toilet is an unpleasant event. This may be because the parents have been too keen for their children to become clean and dry and have told them off and become cross or angry if they have any accidents. This may make the children try to avoid going to the toilet in case they get it wrong.

Attention for accidents

A few children learn that their toileting accidents result in lots of attention. Frustrated parents may spend a lot of time encouraging their children to go to the toilet. Others learn that it is very hard for their parents to ignore a smelly nappy or a pair of wet pants and they may enjoy the one-to-one attention they receive as they are changed. Toileting accidents are a very good way of getting yourself noticed.

IS MY CHILD READY TO USE A POTTY?

The age at which children are able to regularly gain control of their bowels is around two years of age. It does not matter how early you start potty training, most children will not be successful until this age. If you try too early you may become disappointed and you may make your child reluctant to try again at a time when they are more likely to be successful. As a rule of thumb, wait until your child is about two and do not try toilet training before eighteen months at the earliest.

For the majority of children, the process of toilet training involves the child firstly gaining control of their bowels, then their bladder during the daytime, with night-time dryness coming last.

There are no rules for knowing when your child is ready to try potty training. It is all down to trial and error. You may want to try if:

● Your child is two years or older.

● Your child starts to notice when they are weeing and pooing. This means they are tuning in to their body and becoming aware when they are performing.

● Your child shows interest in the potty. If they want to sit on it, then let them try. Do not expect them to be successful at this stage. The important thing is that they are learning to sit in the right place.

● You find that your child has a number of dry or clean nappies when you change them. It may be useful to get them to sit on the potty as you change them to see if they can perform.

If your child refuses to sit on the potty then do not force them. This is probably not the time to start. Put them back into nappies and try again in a few weeks time. It is important to make sure that toileting is a relaxed and positive experience for the child.

TOILET TRAINING

When you start toilet training be prepared for your child to have accidents. They will probably have many wet or dirty pants as they learn to gain control of their bowel or bladder. This is to be expected so do not become cross or upset. Your child is not being naughty.

When you start toilet training:

● Show your child the potty, where it is kept and what it is for. Some children prefer to go straight to the toilet and so you may want to get a child's toilet seat and step to help them get on to the toilet.

● Take their nappy off for part or the whole of the day and put them in pants.

● Encourage them to go and sit on the potty at regular times throughout the day. It is often quite useful to do this about 20 minutes after a meal since this is a time when children are more likely to be able to go.

● If they look as if they are about to go, then gently encourage them to try using the potty.

● Stay with them and provide any help that may be required.

● You may want to make it a special fun time and read a short story whilst your child sits and tries to go.

● If you use a story, then stop occasionally to encourage your child to push.

● Look pleased and praise them if they are successful.

● Never flush the toilet if the child is still sitting on it. This may scare them.

● Most children are very interested in looking at their poos. If they want to look then show them before you flush it down the loo.

● Do not make a fuss about any accidents. Try to ignore these and remind your child that poos and wees are done in the potty.

● Encourage them to wash their hands after they have been to the toilet.

If after a few days you find that your child is not having any success then put their nappy back on. It may not be the right time for them. If they are becoming successful, then keep going.

AVOIDING CONSTIPATION

Constipation is common in children and if a child is constipated they will be unable to gain control of their bowels. To avoid your child becoming constipated the first stage is to make sure that their diet is satisfactory.

● Cut down on milk and sweets since these slow down the movement of the bowels.

● Increase high-fibre foods which help to keep stools soft. Cereals, fruit with skins, jacket potatoes and wholemeal bread are all high-fibre foods.

● Make sure that they are drinking enough, otherwise their faeces will become solid and pellet like.

For older children it is important to make sure that they can get to the toilet when they need to go. It can be frightening for some children to go upstairs on their own to use a toilet and they may try to hold on in order to avoid going. The more they hang on, the more they increase the chance of becoming constipated.

Finally, children need to be reminded to go to the toilet and encouraged to try. For many children sitting on a toilet is low priority and they would much rather be playing with their friends or doing something else. They may try and put off going, holding on to the last minute, which may result in either accidents or your child becoming constipated.

DEALING WITH DAYTIME WETTING

The majority of children do manage to become dry during the day by the time they start playschool. If your child is still having regular daytime accidents then you can help them become dry in the following way.

● Choose a time when you are going to be at home all day.

● Take them out of nappies and try them in pants.

● Show them where the potty is and encourage them to do their wees on it from now on.

● Make sure that your child has lots to drink. Keep offering drinks regularly throughout the day.

● Each hour ask your child to sit on the potty and try and do a wee.

● If they are successful make a big fuss and give them lots of attention and praise.

● For children who are three years old or more, you can use a behaviour chart and give them a star every time they do a wee.

● If they have any accidents then calmly and quickly change their pants. Remind them to do their wees on the potty and ask if they will go and have a try.

● If they do not want to sit on the potty then do not force them, Instead see if you can make it more attractive to try. You could offer to go with them and read a story or play a game.

Other children may be dry during the day most of the time but have occasional accidents. You may want to record when these accidents happen. This may help you see whether there is any pattern and whether they are more likely to occur at certain times. If this is the case then you can try and work out ways in which these can be prevented.

Lucy's wetting
Lucy was three years old. Although she had been dry during the day for about four months she continued to have regular accidents. Her parents did not think this was getting any better and so decided to record every time that Lucy was wet. The diary is shown in Figure 14.

Day and time	Comments
Wednesday 11.05am	Just got to the shops and Lucy wet herself.
Thursday 3.30pm.	Walking back from school after collecting Arthur. Noticed that Lucy was wet.
Sunday 10.30am	Sitting in church at the start of the service and Lucy was wet.
Sunday 2.30pm	Playing in the park and I noticed that Lucy was wet.

Fig. 14. Lucy's wet pants diary

Lucy was not having accidents at any one particular time but the diary did confirm what her parents thought, namely accidents happened while she was out. None of the outings were particularly long and often Lucy was wet fairly soon after leaving the house. Her parents were unsure whether Lucy went to the toilet before she left home and so decided that they would remind her to go before they went out. This simple idea was the answer to Lucy's problems and she became completely dry during the day.

'My child keeps going to the toilet'
Some children visit the toilet many times each day passing small

amounts of wee during each visit. This may be because they are worried and do not want to have any accidents. Try talking to them about it and reassure them that the occasional accident is nothing to worry about.

Other children may have a small functional bladder capacity. This means that they do not completely fill their bladder. Instead they will use only a little and will empty it when only a small amount of wee has built up inside. These children need to learn to use all their bladder so that they go to the toilet less often but do bigger wees.

To help your child do this you can try the following:

● Choose a day when you will be at home

● Give your child regular drinks throughout the day.

● Ask them to tell you when they want to go to the toilet.

● Immediately they tell you they want to go try to get them to wait and hold on.

● For younger children it is best to get them to do something so that they have something else to think about. Play a game, read a story, draw a picture, in fact anything to occupy their mind.

● Older children may enjoy making a game of it. Set a clock and see how long they can wait.

● Once the child has waited and it is clear that they cannot hold on any more then let them go to the toilet.

● Praise them and encourage them to hold on for longer next time and try again.

● Treat any accidents in a calm way.

DEALING WITH NIGHT-TIME WETTING

It is common for pre-school children to wet the bed so it is important not to worry. Since many children become dry as they get older many professionals will not see a child who wets the bed as a problem until they are seven years old.

There are many **false beliefs** about night-time wetting, with the most common being these four:

'Limiting drinks helps children to become dry at night'
Some parents will not give their child drinks after a certain time at night believing that if their child does not drink they will be unable to wet the

bed. Unfortunately this is not the case and limiting drinks does not work. Children who do not have drinks can create more problems since the child's functional bladder capacity may reduce so that they are only able to hold on to smaller amounts of wee before they need to go to the toilet.

'My child is a deep sleeper and so can't wake themself up to go to the toilet'
A common belief about night-time wetting is that some children sleep very heavily and are unable to wake up when their bladder is full. Once again research has proven that this is not the case. Bedwetting can take place at any time during the night and does not just occur in the deepest stage of sleep.

'Lifting my child at night will help them become dry'
A number of parents try lifting their child at night. Lifting involves waking the child once or more after they have gone to bed, placing them on the toilet and encouraging them to wee. Although some parents find this helpful, most do not.

There are a number of problems with lifting.

● You decide when your child goes to the toilet. Your child is not learning to tune into the signals from their bladder which tell them when they need to go to the toilet.

● If your child is not fully awake you may be teaching them to empty their bladder whilst asleep.

● Your child's bladder is unlikely to be full when you lift them. This will not help your child learn the connection between having a full bladder and waking up.

'My child is being deliberately naughty'
Very few children deliberately wet their beds. The overwhelming majority do not. Children who wet the bed are not usually lazy or being wilfully naughty.

Preparing your child to be dry at night
There are some things you can do which will help to prepare your child to become dry at night. These may not have any immediate effect upon your child's bedwetting, but over time they probably will help.

1. Do not restrict drinks during the day or at night. Give them a drink whenever they want one.

2. Avoid giving your child tea, coffee or fizzy drinks before they go to bed. These tend to encourage the bladder to empty.

3. Stop any lifting.

4. Always get your child to go to the toilet before they go to sleep.

5. After they have finished weeing, count to ten and try again. This will make sure that your child fully empties their bladder.

6. Make sure that your child can get to the toilet/potty if they need it.

It may be worth trying at regular times to leave your child's nappy off at night. It is particularly useful to try this if they are waking in the morning with a dry nappy or if they ask for it to be taken off. When you try:

●   Choose a time when you are calm and not too busy. If you are feeling stressed or overwhelmed then it is not the time to try.

●   Cover the mattress with a plastic sheet in case of accidents.

●   Praise any dry beds and make a big fuss of your child.

●   Treat any accidents in a matter of fact sort of way and do not get angry.

●   Expect your child to have accidents, particularly in the early days.

●   If you don't have any success within a week, then put them back in nappies and try again in a couple of months.

DEALING WITH SOILING

Before undertaking any toileting programme it is important to be sure that your child is not constipated. If they are, they will be unable to know when they need to go to the toilet and will be unable to push out what is inside them. Any programme you try will not be successful and both you and your child will have an unnecessary experience of failure.

   If you think your child is constipated then talk about this with your family doctor and wait until your child is clear.

Keeping a toileting diary

Once you are sure that your child is not constipated the next step is to learn more about their accidents. Keeping a toileting diary for a week will be helpful and will give you an idea of:

●   How often your child is emptying their bowel.

- The consistency of their poos. Small pellets or very watery poos are possible signs of constipation.

- When they are most likely to go. This may help you tune in to the time of day when your child is naturally most likely to poo.

- Whether they sit and try to poo regularly throughout the day.

- How you deal with any accidents and how you react if they are successful.

Tim's toileting diary
Tim was three and had never been clean. He had been tried in pants a number of times but he continued to mess himself. His mother, Jane, decided to try again and kept a diary of when Tim went to the loo or had an accident. This is shown in Figure 15.

Day and time	What was happening	What did we do?
Monday 2.00pm	Tim went quiet. Went round the back of the settee, rubbed bottom against settee and pooed pants.	Kept calm, changed him.
Wednesday 1.30pm	After lunch Tim was watching TV. Rubbing his bottom against chair. Found he had done a poo.	Told him to tell me if he wanted to go to the loo. Changed him.
Thursday 3.00pm	Been playing a game in the garden Tim went in and came out ten minutes later. He had pooed his pants.	Went in and changed him.
Friday 1.30pm	Watching TV after lunch. Stood up, went round back of settee and pooed himself.	Kept calm. Asked him to tell me if he wanted to do a poo.

Fig. 15. Tim's toileting diary

Jane was dealing with these accidents in a very calm way but she realised that Tim never sat on the toilet and tried to go. All the accidents were happening in the afternoon and seemed to involve Tim going behind the settee to poo his pants. Jane decided that she would encourage Tim to sit on the toilet each afternoon at 1.00pm, and if he had not pooed then, again at 2.00pm and 3.00pm. If she saw him rubbing himself against the settee or going behind it she would gently take him to the toilet and get him to sit and try. If he was successful Jane made a special fuss of Tim and either read him a story or played a game. The first four days were difficult but after a week Tim started to learn that he went to the toilet when he wanted to poo.

'My child will only poo in his nappy'

Learning to poo in the potty and not the nappy is difficult for some children to learn. A few children become distressed if their nappy is taken away whilst others will insist that it is on before they poo. Some will hold on, refuse to poo and by so doing increase the chance that they will become constipated.

These children have failed to make the transition from pooing in the nappy to pooing in the potty. They can be helped in the following way.

- Take your child's nappy off and put them in pants.

- Encourage and praise them for weeing in the potty.

- When they ask for their nappy or when you think they want to try to poo, put their nappy on but ask them to sit on the potty. Do this a few times so that they get used to the idea of sitting on the potty to poo.

- After this, don't secure the nappy on the child but drape it over the potty. The child will still be pooing into their nappy but it is no longer fastened around them.

- Gradually start to reduce the size of the nappy. Start off by cutting it in half and then make it smaller, but still in/over the potty. Over time the nappy will completely disappear and the child will just be using the potty.

'My child will not poo in the toilet'

Some children will only poo in their pants or somewhere else like behind the settee, or in a corner of the room. They will often happily use the toilet to wee but not to poo. If this happens you need to teach your child that they poo in the toilet and this can be done using the ideas from the earlier section on potty training.

'My child messes herself when I tell her off'

Deliberate messing is not very common but a few children do use their toileting as a way of getting back at their parents. If they have been told off or refused what they want then some children will get their own back by messing their pants or pooing on the carpet or somewhere else. This does not happen very often and you can easily find out if this is the reason by keeping a toileting diary. If the accidents seem to happen after you have told your child off or they have not got their own way then this may be the reason.

In this situation children need to learn that their toileting accidents do not have any positive gains. To do this you could try to:

● Treat any accidents in a calm and neutral way. Do not get cross because this is probably what your child wants you to do.

● Provide any accidents with only little attention. Take them and change them quickly, avoid talking with them, do not make it a game or look pleased.

● Start a behaviour chart for pooing in the toilet. Praise your child whenever they are successful so that they learn that they now get your attention for pooing in the toilet not anywhere else.

● If this doesn't work and you are sure that your child's messing is deliberate then you could introduce a sanction whenever they have an accident. This could be early to bed, not being allowed to watch their favourite TV programme, no sweets, in fact anything that clearly shows your child that their deliberate pooing now has a 'cost' to them.

On other occasions children learn that messing themselves has some positive benefits. They may, for example, be sent home from school or not be allowed to start at playgroup. This may result in them spending time at home which they may enjoy. If this seems to be the case then it is important to:

● Make sure that the potential positive benefits are minimised. If they are sent home then try not to make it too much fun. Don't let them sit and watch their favourite TV programmes. Don't spend all afternoon playing with them or reading stories to them. If home becomes more boring they may become more interested in being at school or playgroup.

● Try to ensure that your child's accidents do not stop you from doing anything. If you want to go out, do so. Take your child, and a few changes of clothes and baby wipes, with you.

● Once again, try a behaviour chart for pooing on the toilet and spend special time with your child, playing, reading, etc., if they are successful. This will help them learn that pooing in the right place has the most advantages and gets your attention.

'My child becomes upset when they go to the toilet'

One a very few occasions children may have had a frightening experience on the toilet. They may have slipped off the toilet seat, been frightened by a barking dog whilst in the loo or been told scary stories about what happens when you sit on the toilet. You will probably find that your child becomes very upset and frightened when they are asked to go to the toilet and they may well stop going there even to wee. In these situations your child needs to be taught that the toilet is not a scary place.

● Think about whether anything unpleasant or scary has happened.

● Talk with your child about what might be scaring them.

● Go with them to the toilet and show them that it is OK.

● Leave the door open if it scares them to shut it.

● Let them see you use the toilet so that they can see it is safe.

● If they are worried about slipping through the toilet seat, then get a smaller child's seat.

● If they are worried about being unable to turn on the light, see if you can fix up a string pull light with a long cord they can reach.

● If the dog barks and scares them, think about where else the dog can go. If the dog can't move then take your chid to the loo and wait until they finish.

● Praise them for going and make a big fuss whenever they are successful.

'My child has occasional accidents'

The majority of children manage to become clean fairly quickly although some will continue to have the occasional accident. This is often nothing to worry about but you may want to keep a diary to find out whether these accidents have a pattern. If they do, try and work out what is worrying your child and how they can be helped to be clean.

'My child holds on until the last minute'

Children would much rather be playing with their friends and toys than sitting on the toilet. Pulling themselves away from something exciting is often difficult, resulting in many leaving it until the very last minute before they rush off to the toilet. Sometimes their pants will be dirty because they have started to poo before they get there. On other occasions it may be because they want to get back quickly and play and may not wipe themselves properly. At these times it will be useful to try and remind your child to go and try. If a friend is coming around to play, encourage them to go to the toilet before they come. If they are watching their favourite TV programmes, encourage them to sit on the toilet either before it starts or during a break.

CASE STUDIES

Leanne always seems to be going to the toilet
Leanne was four and had been toilet trained during the day for the last twelve months. Her parents were worried because Leanne seemed to be constantly on the toilet. She was going to the toilet two or three times every hour and on each occasion she would do a tiny wee. They decided to try and help Leanne to go to the toilet less often.

They had a weekend coming up when they would be at home and decided that this would be a good time to start their plan. Every hour Leanne was offered a drink which she was encouraged to take. These started to fill up her bladder and make her feel a need to go and do a wee. When she wanted to go, her parents asked her to tell them, and then they tried to get Leanne to hold on for as long as possible. They got her to do things such as play games, read stories and do puzzles. When Leanne could hold on no longer she went to the toilet. This was hard for Leanne to start with but as the day went by she could hold on for longer periods of time. Her parents started to record how long she could wait between wees and the time got longer and longer. By the end of the weekend Leanne was going to the toilet only once every hour and a half and was now passing much bigger wees.

Michael has dirty pants
Michael was three and had been taken out of nappies at about two years of age but continued to have dirty pants. His father decided that the time had come to help Michael become completely clean and kept a record of any accidents over the next two weeks. There did not seem to be any particular pattern to Michael's dirty pants. He was taking himself to the loo in time but was in a hurry to get back to his play. His pants were dirty because he was not wiping himself properly. His father taught him to wipe his bottom and when he saw Michael go to the toilet he would

remind him to wipe himself. He also put a picture of a big smiling face by the toilet paper as another reminder and over the next few weeks Michael's pants became clean.

Kamal is constipated

Kamal was three years old and had always found it hard to go to the toilet. He usually did a large poo once a week and often became upset, screaming, crying and saying it 'hurts'. His poos became little dry pellets and he started messing his pants about twice per day. Recently his poos changed and became very runny and smelt awful. Kamal complained of a tummy ache so his parents took him to the doctor, worried that he might have a tummy bug.

Kamal was badly constipated and the recent messing of his pants was caused by faecal overflow. This is where the faeces behind the constipated mass in the tummy become a liquid and start to seep out. The doctor prescribed two lots of medicine. The first softened the compacted faeces in his tummy and the second made Kamal feel an urge to go to the toilet. His parents also made some changes to his diet. They cut down on the amount of milk he drank and made sure that he had more roughage, particularly fresh fruit with skins on and fresh orange juice to drink each morning. This did the trick and within six weeks Kamal was no longer constipated.

DISCUSSION POINTS

1.   What age could you start toilet training your child and how could you help them to become clean and dry.

2.   How would you help your child if they had been dry and had now started to wet themself during the day?

3.   What can you do to help your child become dry at night. What should you encourage and what should you avoid?

6
Coping with Tempers and Defiance

UNDERSTANDING TEMPERS AND DEFIANCE

Temper tantrums

Parents often first notice their children having temper tantrums between nine and fifteen months of age. This is the age when children begin to become more independent and start to crawl or shuffle around on their own. They start to exercise their own will and begin to learn that they can influence what happens and get what they want.

Temper tantrums at this age are often:

● frequent, occurring several times per day

● last only a minute or two

● and children can be fairly easily distracted out of them.

During a temper tantrum, children may:

● throw themselves to the floor

● scream or cry

● say rude or hurtful things (older children)

● throw things

● bite, kick or hit themselves or others

● bang their head on the floor or wall.

As children get older they tend to have less temper tantrums, but they often

● last longer

● may be more extreme or intense

● become harder to distract the child out of.

Most parents find their child has temper tantrums at some stage.

- By the age of two, one in five children will be having at least one temper tantrum each day.

- Approximately one in ten four-year-old children will be having at least one temper tantrum per day.

- On many occasions the tantrum will be triggered by the child being unable to get their own way or by the word 'No'.

Dealing with tempers can be difficult and about one in five parents are concerned about how to deal with their child's tantrums.

Non-compliance, defiance, answering back

As children become more independent they start to challenge their parents, test the rules and limits and increasingly try to do what they want. Defiance and non-compliance are common in pre-school children.

Non-compliance and defiance may take many different forms, including:

- saying 'No'

- arguing or answering back

- constantly questioning 'Why' something can't happen

- shouting, saying unkind things or calling people names

- ignoring parental requests

- continuing to do as they want

- repeatedly doing the same thing when they have been told to stop.

About one in four parents are concerned about how to deal with their child's defiant and challenging behaviour.

COMMON CAUSES OF TEMPERS AND DEFIANCE

Temper tantrums and defiance are a normal part of childhood development and most children will act this way at some time or another. There are many reasons why this may happen, with the main ones being:

- frustration

- wanting attention

- being tired, hungry or temperamentally difficult
- worry or uncertainty
- children learning that they get what they want.

Expressing frustration

As children get older they are keen to explore their world, to learn, and to start to do things their way. They are unaware that certain things are dangerous or simply not allowed. If they are prevented from doing these things or told 'No', they may become angry or frustrated and throw a tantrum. For many children, temper tantrums are their way of expressing their feelings of frustration.

Getting attention

Temper tantrums and defiance are a good way of getting noticed. It is hard to ignore a child who is screaming or crying or a child who just continues doing as they wish. Defiance and tempers often result in parents getting sucked into long drawn out discussions with their children. Attempting to reason with them at this time is usually unsuccessful and often makes matters worse. Some children learn that tempers and defiance are a good way of getting adult attention.

Being tired, hungry or temperamentally difficult

Tantrums, particularly in young children, are more likely to occur around mealtimes or bedtimes. Children who are hungry or tired may become irritable and show this by having temper tantrums.

Other children may be temperamentally difficult and more likely to challenge, question and push the limits. These differences have been noticed in very young babies. Some babies are very easy going, regular in their eating and sleeping patterns, positive in their mood, adapting quickly and easily to change. Others are more active, irregular in their eating and sleep, more unsettled in their mood, and find it harder to cope with change.

Expressing worry or uncertainty

Children are not always able to talk about their feelings or discuss their worries and often their behaviour is a sign that they are afraid or anxious. They may have more tempers or become defiant if they are unsettled or worried particularly at times of uncertainty. This is a way of checking that the rules are still there even if other things have changed. With this comes a sense of security, predictability, and certainty that everything will be alright.

Children learning that they get what they want

Children learn from an early age that what they do and how they behave has an effect, i.e. it results in some sort of consequences. For some children, having a temper tantrum may get them what they want. A child may initially be refused an ice cream but when they scream and cry their parent gives in to calm them down. In this case the child will learn that having a temper is a good way of getting what they want. Similarly, a child who ignores their parent may learn that they can do as they wish.

DEALING WITH DEFIANCE

A defiant child is very frustrating and tiring for parents to deal with. Rather than constantly arguing with your child a more useful approach is to think about how they can be helped to become more co-operative.

Encouraging children to co-operate

Parents often give their children requests which almost encourage them to play up or be defiant. Try and avoid this and think about the following:

Using positive instructions
Wherever possible, try and use positive instructions. Avoid setting yourself up for failure by saying things like:

● 'I don't suppose you want to go to bed yet.'

● 'You always play up when we go out.'

● 'Tom, you just can't behave yourself.'

These statements almost encourage children to defy you and suggest that you are expecting them to misbehave. This can be avoided by using clear, positive, encouraging statements which tell the child how you would like them to behave.

● 'Mike, it's time for bed.'

● 'Sara, I want you to hold my hand when we go to the shops.'

● 'Tom, I would like you to sit quietly on the settee, please.'

Only giving 'real' choices
Sometimes parents give their child a choice when the child doesn't really have one.

- A parent needs to go to the shops but says to their child, 'shall we go to the shops?'

- A parent asks their child, 'do you think fishfingers would be nice for tea?' when tea has already been bought.

Asking questions when the child doesn't really have a choice increases the chance that they will want to do things differently. Understandably this will make them feel frustrated, angry and defiant when you impose your own will.

Prompting children to behave well
In many families the rules are not always clear. Children only find out that they have done wrong after they have misbehaved. At other times parents avoid reminding their children to behave well, fearing that this will make them more likely to play up. A more positive approach is to make it very clear what will happen and how you want them to behave.

- Before a friend comes to play, remind your child to share their toys.

- Before you go to the shops, remind your child to hold your hand.

- Tell your child five minutes before you leave that you will soon be going home.

Praising children for doing as you have asked
Children often receive a great deal of attention for misbehaving whilst parents rarely praise them for doing as they are asked. Many parents simply expect their child to do as they are told.

   Help your child learn that they receive your attention and praise for behaving well and that their compliance is noticed.

- Praise them at regular times for doing as they have been asked.

- Use a behaviour chart, as discussed earlier. The child can earn stickers for doing as they have been asked.

Following 'jobs' with something enjoyable
A useful way of encouraging children to follow requests is to arrange to do something enjoyable after they have done what you have asked.

- 'Haseem, please pick up your books and then we will have a biscuit.'

- 'Mary, after we go to the shops we will stop off at the park.'

- 'John, if you get dressed quickly we will have time to look in the toy shop.'

Arranging pleasant things to follow 'jobs' increases the chance that children will do as you ask.

Avoiding direct confrontations

Many parents complain that their children are more likely to be defiant if they directly ask them to do something. They feel that their children immediately reply 'No'. At these times it is useful to avoid directly asking children to do things. Try using a more indirect approach instead.

- Ask your child to help you get a drink from the kitchen rather than telling them to leave the TV changer alone. Your request has served the same purpose and has got them away from messing with the TV.

- Ask a child who is jumping on the furniture and running around to sit and listen to a story rather than asking them to calm down.

- Make a game of clearing away the toys. Try asking, 'I wonder how quickly you can put these in the box?' rather than directly asking your child to tidy up their toys.

Indirect methods can be very useful, particularly for those children who tend to immediately say 'No' to any request.

Ignoring minor defiance

Parents often feel that they are arguing with their children or constantly telling them off. Many of these arguments are about small or unimportant things or about the child doing things differently from what their parent would like.

- Instead of putting toys in the box one by one, they may scoop a number up and drop them in together.

- They may say 'No' but then do as you ask.

- They may moan and argue as they get on with what you have requested.

On these occasions it is important not to make any critical comments or pay any attention to what the child is saying. This often increases the chance of a bigger argument developing and increases the number of critical messages your child hears. Your child is doing as you have asked even if they aren't doing it in the way you would like.

Adopting the 1, 2, 3 approach

At other times it is important that your child does as you ask. On these occasions, parents need to firmly and consistently enforce what they have requested. They need to make sure that their child does as they ask without repeating requests time and time again. The 1, 2, 3 approach, described in Figure 16, is a very useful way of avoiding giving endless instructions.

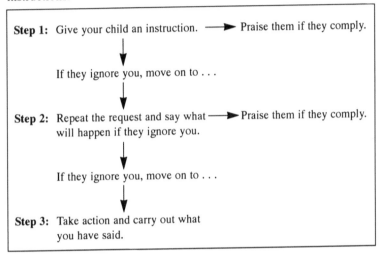

Step 1: Give your child an instruction. ——► Praise them if they comply.

If they ignore you, move on to . . .

Step 2: Repeat the request and say what ——► Praise them if they comply.
will happen if they ignore you.

If they ignore you, move on to . . .

Step 3: Take action and carry out what
you have said.

Fig. 16. The 1, 2, 3 approach.

This is a very useful way of dealing with non-compliance. The method:

● provides a clear framework for children and parents

● prevents parents making endless requests

● minimises the amount of attention children receive for misbehaving

● ensures that parents are consistent and follow things through.

COPING WITH TEMPERS

Keeping a temper diary

Temper tantrums are common and can occur for many different reasons. It is useful to find out if your child's tempers fall into a particular pattern and a diary is one way of checking this.

Winston's temper diary
Winston was two and seemed to his parents to be having a lot of temper

tantrums. They decided to keep a diary and wrote down whenever Winston had a tantrum. The diary is shown in Figure 17.

Day and time	What was happening?	What did we do?
Monday 9.30am	Turned the TV off. Winston had a tantrum.	Left TV off and walked away. Winston calm in about one minute.
Monday 10.25am	In the shop, Winston wanted a pack of sweets. Said No, he had a tantrum.	Winston continued to cry. I felt embarrassed and gave him the sweets. Winston was calm.
Monday 12.00	Told Winston to come for dinner. He was watching TV and refused. I turned it off and he screamed and yelled.	Ignored him for five minutes then put the TV on to calm him down. He went quiet. Let him eat his dinner in front of TV.
Monday 3.00pm	Getting ready to go to the shops. Winston didn't want to go. Had temper.	Put his coat on and put him in the buggy. Calm by time got outside.
Monday 4.30pm	Winston wanted a biscuit. I said No, soon be tea time. Winston screamed.	I was talking to my friend so got him a biscuit so that we could hear ourselves talk.

Fig. 17. Winston's temper diary.

The diary helped Winston's parents learn that they did not always stick with what they said and sometimes gave in. Winston had learned that his tempers often resulted in him getting what he wanted.

Winston's parents decided that they had to become more consistent and agreed that they would no longer give in to any of his demands. This would help Winston learn that tempers did not result in him getting his own way.

Preventing tantrums

Most parents know that there are certain times when their children are more likely to have temper tantrums. This may be:

● whilst walking home after nursery

● when a certain friend comes to play

- when they are asked to get dressed in the morning

- when the television is turned off.

If there are things which are more likely to trigger temper outbursts, then it may be useful to think about how these can be prevented. It may be that you could:

- arrange for someone else to walk home with you from nursery to keep your child occupied

- remind your child before the friend comes to play to try and keep calm

- start a behaviour chart for dressing in the morning

- arrange for something nice or interesting to happen after the TV is turned off.

Be prepared to experiment. Try to do things differently and see if the tantrums can be prevented.

Ignoring minor tantrums

One of the best ways of dealing with a child who is having a minor temper tantrum is to ignore them. Most minor tantrums involve children crying, shouting or screaming or just repeating themselves time and time again.

On these occasions, avoid:

- Trying to talk the child out of it. This gives them a lot of attention and in many cases tends to make the tantrum last longer.

- Asking them what is the matter. Many children will be unable to tell you why they are cross and this becomes more frustrating for both the child and their parent.

- Getting into long drawn out arguments or explanations about why they cannot have what they want. This is the wrong time. The child is angry, is not rational, and will be unable to listen to and understand reasoned arguments.

Instead, make sure that the child is safe and cannot hurt themself and leave them to it. Try not to look at them or make any comments about the temper and move away until the child is calm.

Using 'time out' for aggression

If a child becomes physically aggressive during a temper they need a clear message that this sort of behaviour is not acceptable. They need to receive a consequence that has a 'cost' which will help them learn that acting in such a way is unacceptable. Of the consequences available, 'time out' is most effective for young children. This method was described in Chapter 2 and involves withdrawing attention from the child for a short period of time, immediately they misbehave.

● Tell them clearly and simply that what they have done is unacceptable, e.g. 'Simon, we do not kick other people.'

● *Either*:
Send them to a 'time out' place, e.g. special chair in the corner of the room, bottom of the stairs, their bedroom.
Or:
Withdraw your attention by walking away, doing something else, etc.

● 'Time out' should last about two minutes and definitely no longer than three minutes.

● Repeat every time they are aggressive.

'What if they play up when we go out'

A child misbehaving in public is a situation most parents dread and find very difficult to deal with. Parents often do not know how to cope with such a situation and feel that they are being watched and criticised by others. This situation cannot always be avoided, but sometimes you can reduce the chance of it happening.

Before you go out:

● Make sure the trip is manageable and not too long. If you are planning to go shopping for three hours, work out how it can be broken up so that there are things for your child to do, e.g. have a drink in a café, visit the toy shop, feed the birds, etc.

● Remind your child how you would like them to behave. Do this before you leave the house and at regular times throughout the trip.

● Arrange for something nice to happen at the end of the trip if your child has behaved well. Tell them this before you go.

Whilst you are out:

- Provide your child with feedback about how they are doing at regular times. Praise them for behaving well.

- You could carry a small behaviour chart with you and draw on smiley faces after every 15 or 30 minutes for behaving well.

- Work out how you can involve your children to stop them from getting bored, e.g. get them to help put shopping in the basket, etc.

If they do play up:

- Try to keep calm and be firm.

- If your child is crying or screaming then take them somewhere that is less crowded, e.g. a quiet part of the shop or a side street, and wait there until they calm down.

- If you travelled in a car you could take them back to the car park and make them sit in the car until they are calm. You can then continue with your trip.

- Do not give in to their demands or try to bribe them with treats to calm down. This will only increase the chance that they will play up on your next outing.

- Remember that you know best. You know your child better than anyone else and know why they are misbehaving and how you want to deal with it. Thinking clearly like this will increase your confidence and you will feel less bothered by comments from others.

'What about smacking?'

Parents often wonder whether they should smack their children for more serious misbehaviour, feeling that 'time out' is not a big enough consequence. There is, however, no evidence to suggest that smacking is useful. Research has found that smacking:

- is ineffective – has no long-term benefits

- sends a confusing message to the child – it is wrong for you to hit your friend but right for me to smack you

- becomes more severe as children get older

- teaches children to use aggression – they learn that this is the way to sort out disagreements.

Often parents smack children in desperation because they do not know what else to do. Having a clear 'time out' strategy is helpful and provides both parents and children with a chance to calm down.

CASE STUDIES

Layla's parents use the 1, 2, 3 approach

Layla was four and seemed to ignore whatever her parents asked her to do. Her parents had not always been consistent and had often let her get away with things. With school approaching they decided that they needed to teach Layla that she had to do as she was asked and decided to use the 1, 2, 3 approach.

Before they went out to the shops, her mother asked, 'Layla, would you pick up your bricks, please?' Layla carried on playing, and after about fifteen seconds her mother repeated the request. 'Layla, this is number two. Please pick up your bricks otherwise you will sit on the step.' Layla ignored her mother and after a few minutes she said, 'Layla, you have to do as you are asked. Sit on the step'. Layla refused and so she was taken by her mother to the step where she stayed for two minutes.

Later in the day they went out shopping and Layla kept running off. Her mother asked, 'Layla, please hold my hand'. Layla refused and so her mother repeated her request. 'Layla, this is number two. Please hold my hand otherwise I will hold yours.' Layla attempted to run off but her mother caught her and held on firmly to her hand for the rest of the trip.

Later in the evening Layla was asked to get into her pyjamas. Layla carried on playing with her dolls. After a minute her father repeated the request saying, 'Layla, this is number two. Please get into your pyjamas otherwise there will be no story tonight'. Layla then went and got herself ready for bed. Her father praised Layla for doing as she was asked and read her the story.

Holly goes to 'time out'

Over the past two months, three-year-old Holly had started to bite other children. Her parents had dealt with this biting in different ways including telling her off, stopping sweets and smacking her. This didn't seem to be working and Holly continued to bite other children about four times per week.

Holly's parents decided to use a different approach and agreed to send her to 'time out' whenever she bit. At home they had a chair they could put facing the corner and a similar arrangements could be used at nursery. Holly's parents talked with her about the biting. They told her that it was unkind and explained that from now on she would sit in the corner for two minutes whenever she bit.

For the first week there was no biting but at the start of the second week she bit her brother. Her father saw this happen and said very firmly, 'Holly, you do not hurt others. Sit on the chair.' Holly went and stayed there for two minutes whilst her father cuddled and calmed his son. After two minutes Holly joined in playing again. Her father did not go on about what she had done. Holly received little attention for behaving this way and had a very clear message that this was unacceptable. Later that week she bit a friend who came to play and once again she received a clear message. 'Holly, you do not bite. Sit on the chair.' This time Holly refused to go. Her mother did not get into an argument about this but firmly took Holly to the corner and put her in the chair. Holly tried to get up and run away but her mother stood behind the chair and gently but firmly pushed down on her shoulders so that she couldn't run off. She did not talk or argue with Holly, did not look at her, and eventually Holly sat quietly for two minutes. At the end of this time she joined in playing with the others. This process was repeated every time Holly bit.

Imran plays up when out with his parents
Imran was four and was very difficult each week when he went shopping with his parents. He would run around the supermarket picking things up and would scream and demand sweets on the way out. Recently another shopper made some very loud and critical comments about Imran's behaviour which upset his parents and made them decide that something had to be done.

The next time they went shopping they talked with Imran and asked him to hold the shopping trolley when they were in the supermarket. They told him that if he did this he could have some sweets on the way home. Before they went into the supermarket they reminded Imran about this again. Whilst walking around the shop they praised him every few minutes for staying with them and for not touching. They involved Imran by helping him to count the number of things they were buying. The trip was successful and Imran was rewarded with some sweets on the way home.

DISCUSSION POINTS

1. Think about the times when your child is most likely to be defiant or have tantrums. Is there anything you could do differently which may prevent these from happening?

2. How can you stop arguing with your child or constantly picking up
    on their more minor misbehaviour? What would help you to
    become better at ignoring this?

3. How can you remind yourself to praise your children more often for
    doing as you ask?

7
Planning to Change the Way your Child Behaves

Difficult and demanding behaviour in young children is common and most toddlers will behave this way at some time or another. A number of these difficulties will:

● be on-off events

● be a short phase the child is going through

● occur at a time of change

● indicate stress or worry within the family.

In many cases these problems will quickly sort themselves out and parents do not have to actively try and change the way their child behaves or how they react.

IS THIS A PROBLEM YOU NEED TO CHANGE?

Because difficulties come and go the first thing you need to decide is whether your child's behaviour really is a problem that you need to actively attempt to change. You may find it helpful to ask yourself the following questions:

● Is this a long-term difficulty or has it recently started?

● Does it happen often or only occasionally?

● Does it have a significant effect on the child or your family?

● Has there been any change that may have caused your child to behave this way?

● Is your child worried about anything that might have unsettled them?

● Is it really your child's problem or is your child's behaviour a sign of stress or worry within your family?

These questions will help you understand what is happening and help you decide what you need to do.

Annoying behaviour or a major problem?

Children do many things that their parents would prefer they didn't. Whilst these might be irritating and annoying, many are comparatively minor. Trying to change these 'irritants' is unnecessary and unhelpful and may result in you constantly correcting your child. You will probably feel that you are always telling them off, whilst your child will hear more critical messages which may make them think that they cannot do anything right.

To avoid this it is useful to think about all your child's difficult behaviour and to write this down clearly on a piece of paper. Once you have identified all the difficulties decide which is the most important and concentrate on this. Ignore the less important irritating behaviours and try to live with them rather than changing them.

Assessing the costs of change

Trying to change the way your child behaves or how you deal with them is not always easy.

● You may worry or find it distressing to leave your child to cry themselves to sleep.

● Your child may become upset and angry as they understand and accept the new rules.

● You may argue or disagree with your partner or relatives about what should be done.

● Grandparents or friends may criticise what you do.

These are some of the 'costs of change' that need to be thought about before you decide to try and alter what is happening. For some, the 'costs of change' are greater than the 'costs of living with' what is currently happening. If this is the case, it is better to wait until you are able to cope with these 'costs'. Trying to do things before you are ready will probably result in you being unsuccessful.

THINKING ABOUT THE PRACTICAL CONSIDERATIONS

If you decide that your child is showing behaviour which you want to change, it is important to think about the following practical points.

Working on one thing at a time

Children often have a number of problems and there is a temptation for parents to want to try and change everything at the same time. They may, for example, want to improve their child's mealtime behaviour, their sleeping pattern and their level of co-operation. Trying this has both advantages and disadvantages.

Advantages

● Tackling everything may result in quicker improvements.

● There is a feeling that everything is being sorted out.

Disadvantages

● You may become overwhelmed and exhausted by your efforts.

● You may spread your efforts too thinly and do nothing well.

In order to increase the chance of success it is useful to work on one difficulty at a time. Tackling one problem allows you to concentrate all your efforts on that particular difficulty. This will help you be firmer and more consistent which will help your child to quickly learn how they should behave.

Telling your child how you want them to behave

Parents often tell their children what they want them to stop doing but are not always good at telling them how they want them to behave instead. For everything you want to discourage there is more appropriate behaviour you wish to encourage.

● 'Stop messing with your food' could become 'Michael, please use your spoon.'

● 'Don't run off' could become 'Jane, walk with me and hold my hand.'

● 'No hitting' could become 'Jade, I want you to be kind to Jessie.'

Positive instructions tell children very clearly how you would like them to behave.

Choosing the right time to start

If you decide that you want to introduce a plan to teach your child to behave differently, it is important to choose the right time to start.

- If you have a series of important meetings at work and need your sleep, wait until these have finished before you try and help your child to sleep through the night.

- If you will be out of your home a great deal, do not try to start toilet training. Wait until you have a few clear days at home so that you can leave the nappies off and help your child get into a toileting routine.

- If you are feeling particularly tired, it is not the right time to try and tackle your child's defiance.

Choosing the right time rather than rushing straight in to something will increase the chance that your plan is successful.

Making the plan right for the family
The plan needs to be agreed and supported by all the key people who might be involved. This will ensure that your child:

- is treated in a consistent way

- receives the same message from their adult carers

- learns that behaving this way is important and noticed by different people.

If this is not done your child may become confused about how they are expected to behave. To avoid this:

- Parents need to agree and feel comfortable with the plan so that they can support each other.

- The plan has to be built around what they can and cannot do. There is no point in saying that uneaten food will be put in the bin after fifteen minutes if you cannot do it.

- The plan has to reflect parental beliefs about parenting. If one parent does not believe in giving children special rewards for behaving well, do not use a reward programme.

- If relatives or friends ignore your plan, try and avoid them being involved with your child, at least for a short while.

Within families there may be more than one child and parents are often keen for children to be treated in a similar way. Older children may question why, for example, their youngest brother has a special chart for sleeping at night when they already sleep well but do not have a chart.

- You can use reward programmes for all your children if you wish.

- Each will have their own individual target depending upon what behaviour you wish to encourage.

- The principle of encouraging and praising good behaviour can be applied to all children.

Getting support for you
Trying to change the way your child behaves and how you react to them is stressful.

- There will be a number of 'costs of change' that have to be coped with.

- During the difficult times, parents will question and doubt whether they are doing the right thing.

- There will be times when parents will consider giving up.

- Often parents start with enthusiasm but over time their determination begins to fade.

Parents need support to cope with this stress and encouragement to continue with their plans. Before you start, it is useful to think about who may be able to provide this support.

- If you have a partner, discuss and agree with them how you can help each other.

- If your partner is unsupportive or if you are on your own, identify a good friend or relative who can help.

- Talk with them about what you are planning to do and arrange to meet or telephone them shortly after you have started to discuss how it has gone.

- Make sure that you have regular opportunities to talk about how things are going, particularly in the early stages.

PLANNING THE PROGRAMME

1. Praise children for behaving well
Children need to receive adult attention, praise or special treats for

behaving well. They need to learn that their good behaviour gets them noticed and that behaving this way has advantages.

Make it clear to your child how you would like them to behave and praise them when they do. You can make this connection very clear by using the behaviour charts or reward programmes that we discussed in Chapter 2.

2. Give children little attention for misbehaving

Many children learn that they get noticed and receive adult attention when they play up. This needs to be avoided so make sure that your child's minor misbehaviour is ignored and that more serious incidents are dealt with in a firm and consistent way as we discussed in Chapter 2.

3. Be consistent

Make sure that you react to your child's behaviour in a consistent way. If you are erratic your child will become confused and unsure about what they should be doing.

4. Stick with it

Once you have decided to try something new, stick with it. Often difficulties seem to get worse when you try to do things differently and this is a time when many parents question what they are doing and give up. This is a common pattern, so stick with it and you will probably find that things will improve.

5. Keep a diary

A diary is a useful way of keeping check on how things are going. Often change is small and may take time. Your child will probably continue to have temper tantrums but perhaps they happen less often or are shorter. A diary can help you see this progress and is particularly useful at those times when you are doubting what you are doing.

If the diary shows that things are not improving, it may be useful to talk about this with your health visitor or family doctor.

6. Have fun

An important part of being a parent is to enjoy your children and have fun together. It is important not to lose sight of this and to make time to sit down and play and enjoy each other.

CASE STUDIES

The costs of changing Mark's sleeping arrangements

Mark was three and had always slept in his parents' bed. His parents were becoming unhappy with this arrangement and wondered whether they should try to teach Mark to sleep in his own room. They worked out how they would try and do this and then thought about the difficulties that might arise. They identified the following 'costs of change':

1. Mark would probably cry when they started their plan. In the past he had cried for up to forty minutes and so his parents were worried that he would work himself up to a very distressed state.

2. Mark would probably keep coming out of his bedroom and try to get in with his parents. This would need his parents to be firm and to keep taking him back to his own room, something they thought would be difficult after the first three or four times.

3. The family would probably have some disrupted nights sleep whilst Mark learned to sleep on his own. They would become tired.

4. Both parents found it very hard to leave their children to cry and felt unsure whether they could stick with their plan.

5. The neighbours might be woken and relationships with them at the moment were not good.

Mark's parents decided that, although they would prefer their son to sleep in his own room, the costs of change were too great. This was not the time to tackle this problem. They waited for another nine months until they felt ready, determined and able to carry out their plan. By this stage the costs of change were less and they successfully taught Mark to sleep on his own.

Joe's irritating behaviour

Four-year-old Joe had a number of habits which his mother found very annoying. When Joe was asked to do something he would immediately reply 'No' although he always then went and did as he was asked. After a particularly difficult day when Joe had seemed to say 'No' all day, his mother decided things had to change. She drew up the following list of all the things Joe needed to learn:

To get himself dressed.
To do as asked without saying 'No'.
To use a knife and fork.
To drink from different cups.
To poo in the toilet not his pants.

Joe's mother prioritised which of these was the most important and decided that Joe needed to learn to poo on the toilet. Joe was due to start school in two months and she was worried that he might be teased by the other children. The list helped her recognise which problem she needed to concentrate on and that in general Joe was a very co-operative boy. His initial reaction of saying 'No' to her requests was very annoying but she decided to ignore it rather than actively attempting to stop it.

Tashi's bedtime routine

Tashi was put to bed by her mother on three nights per week and by her father for the remaining four. Her parents had different routines so that her mother put her to bed at 7.00 whilst her father would leave her until about 8.30. After one very difficult evening when Tashi refused to go to bed, her mother decided that they had to work out a bedtime plan. Her father thought that 7.00 was too early and so they agreed that Tashi would go to bed at 8.00. Tashi's mother was keen to introduce a reward programme if Tashi went to bed when told. Tashi's father was unhappy about this unless they could do something similar for their five-year-old son. They felt that his behaviour at mealtimes could be improved and so both children were started on reward programmes.

The parents agreed a plan which they both felt comfortable with and able to carry out and in which both children were treated the same.

DISCUSSION POINTS

1. What support would you need if you tried to change your child's behaviour and who would be able to provide this?

2. List the fun things you and your child do together. Does the amount of 'fun time' seem right and how could you increase it?

3. What is the most important behaviour you would like to improve and what would be the 'costs' of trying to change it?

Glossary

Attention. Showing your child that you have noticed what they do by looking at or talking with them.

Behaviour chart. A way of making clear to your child how you would like them to behave. Often called star or reward charts.

Child psychologist. A qualified professional who specialises in understanding how children develop, think, behave and learn.

Consequences. What happens immediately after your child behaves in a certain way.

Consistent. Behaving the same way every time something happens.

Constipation. Difficulty or inability to poo.

Controlled crying. Leaving your child to cry for a fixed time before checking them.

Costs of change. All the things involved in trying to do something differently.

Defiance. Constantly ignoring or doing the opposite of what has been asked.

Diary. A written record of what has happened.

Distraction. Encouraging the child to take their mind off of what is going on by thinking about or doing something else.

Family doctor. General Practitioner (GP).

Health visitor. A qualified community nurse who understands children and the worries they create for their families.

Ignoring. Not looking at or talking with a child who is misbehaving.

Negative consequences. What happens after your child behaves in a certain way that decreases the chance of this happening again.

Nightmares. Bad dreams that usually wake the child.

Night terror. A deep stage of sleep during which a child can talk, walk and thrash about.

Paediatrician. A qualified doctor who specialises in working with children.

Positive consequences. Things that your child finds enjoyable that will increase the chance that they will behave in a certain way again.

Positive instruction. Telling your child how you would like them to behave.

Praise. Showing your child that you are pleased with what they have done by saying nice things, looking pleased or by giving them a hug or cuddle.

Prompting. Encouraging children to behave well.

Reward programme. A way of linking how your child behaves with a special treat.

Rules. Limits that clearly tell your child what is acceptable and what is not.

Situation. When and where did it happen, who was there and what did they do.

Soiling. Pooing in pants or somewhere other than the potty or toilet.

Sleep cues. Things that your child associates with going to sleep.

Target. A clearly defined behaviour that you want to learn more about or change.

Time out. A way of dealing with misbehaviour that involves safely withdrawing attention from the child for a couple of minutes.

Weaning. Encouraging a baby to have less milk feeds and more solid foods.

Further Reading

For parents

My Child Won't Sleep, Jo Douglas and Naomi Richman (Penguin).

The Sleep Book for Tired Parents, Rebecca Huntley (Souvenir Press).

The Baby and Toddler Sleep Programme, John Pearce (Vermillion).

Solve your Child's Sleep Problems, Richard Feber (Dorling Kindersley).

Bedwetting: a Guide for Parents (Enuresis Research & Information Centre).

Help your Child to Sleep, Robyn Pound (Millstream Books).

Coping with Young Children, Jo Douglas and Naomi Richman (Penguin).

Toddler Taming, Christopher Green (Vermillion).

501 Ways to be a Good Parent, Michele Elliott (Hodder & Stoughton).

The Heart of Parenting, John Gottman (Bloomsbury).

How to Succeed as a Parent, Steve Chalke (Hodder & Stoughton).

Practical Parenting, Glen Stenhouse, (Oxford University Press).

Your New Baby, Christine and Peter Hill, (Vermillion).

The New Baby Care Book, Miriam Stoppard, (Dorling Kindersley).

What to Expect: the Toddler Years, Arlene Eisenberg, Heidi Murkoff and Sardee Hathaway, (Simon & Schuster Ltd).

Children's Problems: a Parents' Guide to Understanding and Tackling Them, Bryan Lask (Dunitz).

For professionals

Behaviour Problems in Young Children: Assessment and Management, Jo Douglas (Tavistock/Routledge).

Parent, Adolescent and Child Training Skills, Martin Herbert (British Psychological Society).

Behavioural Treatment of Problem Children: a Practice Manual, Martin Herbert, (Academic Press).

Childhood Behaviour Problems, R. McAuley and P. McAuley, (Macmillan).

Helping the Non-compliant Child: a Clinician's Guide to Parent Training, R. Forehand, R. McMahon, (Guilford).

Coercive Family Process: a Social Learning Approach, G. Patterson (Castalia).

Emotional and Behavioural Problems in Young Children: a Multi-disciplinary Approach to Identification and Management, Jo Douglas (NFER/Nelson).

Troubled Families: Problem Children, Carolyn Webster-Stratton and Martin Herbert (Wiley).

Defiant Children: a Clinician's Manual for Parent Training, Russell Barkley (Guilford).

Children's books

These are story books for children which provide a fun way of helping parents and children understand and talk about common problems.

Books about sleep:

Can't you Sleep Little Bear? Martin Waddell and Barbara Firth (Walker).

Bedtime for Bear, Sandol Stoddard (Hodder & Stoughton).

There's a Nightmare in my Cupboard, M. Mayer (Penguin).

We're Not Tired, Selina Young (Mammoth).

The Owl who was Afraid of the Dark, J. Tomlinson, (Macmillan).

Books about tempers and the determination of children:

Angry Arthur, Hiawyn Oram (Red Fox Picture Books).

I Want a Cat, T. Ross (Red Fox Picture Books).

The trials of potty training:

I Want my Potty, Tony Ross (Red Fox Picture Books).

How adults are not always very good at listening to or noticing their children:

Not Now Bernard, David Mckee (Red Fix Picture Books).

There's No Such Thing as a Dragon, Jack Kent (Blackie).

How children find it difficult to admit what they have done:

Oscar Got the Blame, Tony Ross (Red Fox Picture Books)

How children often find things hard until they become a game:

Well I Never, Heather Eyles and Tony Ross (Red Fox Picture Books).

Useful Addresses

The British Psychological Society, St Andrews House, 48 Princess Road East, Leicester LE1 7DR. Tel: (0116) 254 9568. Professional organisation providing advice on how to find an appropriately qualified psychologist.

The Child Psychotherapy Trust, Star House, 104–108 Grafton Road, London NW5 4BD. Tel: (0171) 284 1355. Professional organisation for child psychotherapists.

Young Minds, 2nd Floor, 102–108 Clerkenwell Road, London EC1M 5SA. Tel: (0171) 336 8445. Parents Information Service: 0345 626376. Information service for parents about local child and family services.

Parentline, Endway House, The Endway, Hadleigh, Essex SS7 2AN. Tel: (01702) 559900. A national helpline for anyone who is finding parenting difficult.

Parent Network, 44–46 Caversham Road, London NW5 2DS. Tel: (0171) 485 8538. Offers Parent-Link support and education groups for parents to talk about the problems of family life.

Exploring Parenthood, 4 Ivory Place, 20A Treadgold Street, London W11 4BP. Tel: (0171) 221 6681. National advice and counselling service for parents aiming to help them find ways of coping with the stresses and strains of everyday life.

National Childbirth Trust, Alexandra House, Oldham Terrace, Acton, London W3 6NH. Tel: (0171) 992 8637. Help, advice and support for mothers, providing antenatal classes and postnatal groups.

Gingerbread, 16–17 Clerkenwell Close, London EC1R 0AA. Tel: (0171) 336 8184. Emotional support, practical help and social activities for lone parents.

Home-Start, 2 Salisbury Road, Leicester LE1 7QR. Tel: (0116) 233 9955. Volunteers who are parents themselves visit families with at least one child under five who are experiencing difficulties.

Kidscape, 152 Buckingham Palace Road, London SW1W 9TR. Tel:

(0171) 730 3300. Provides a range of booklets on bullying, keeping safe and child abuse.

National Council for One Parent Families, 255 Kentish Town Road, London NW5 2LX. Tel: (0171) 267 1361. Free information for one parent families on financial, legal and housing problems.

Childline, Freepost 1111, London N1 0BR. Tel: 0800 1111. Free 24-hour national helpline for children with problems.

National Stepfamily Association, Chapel House, 18 Hatton Place, London EC1 8RU. Tel: (0990) 168 388. Advice, information and counselling services for stepfamilies.

Index

HELPING YOUR CHILD TO READ
How to prepare the child of today for the world tomorrow

Jonathan Myers

Would you like your child to be able to read well? How do you support your child's reading, at school and at home? Who do you ask for advice? What games and activities are useful? What should you look for when buying books? When does a reading problem need expert attention? How do you check your child's progress? In our fast moving, computerised world, reading is absolutely vital. It is the key basic skill that children and adults need to transmit information. And reading is fun too. With its lively text, examples and case studies, this forward looking book shows how easy it is for you to get your child on the right road to reading success. Jonathan Myers BSc PGCE is an educational consultant and teacher specialising in reading development, dyslexia and a wide range of associated problems.

141pp. illus. 1 85703 192 X.

SUCCESSFUL GRANDPARENTING
How to manage family relationships and practical issues

Doris Corti

The average life expectancy is increasing. More people are likely to experience the joys and sorrows of being a grandparent for a longer period of their life. Being a grandparent is different from being a parent. Expectations are different. Many grandparents find that the requirements for bringing up children in today's changing world are very different from what was the norm when they were parents. This book gives practical advice on such diverse aspect as finances, housing, child-minding, taking the role of step-grandparent, sharing grandchildren's upbringing, diplomacy, and obtaining access to children when parents separate or divorce. The answers to these and other problems are given in this book, as well as the names and addresses of helpful organisations. As well as grandparents, typical readers of this book will include grandparents-to-be, retirement groups, library readers, counsellors in church organisations and citizens advice bureaux. Doris Corti has three grandchildren and is an active member of the Grandparents Association.

112pp. illus. 1 85703 307 8.

SUCCESSFUL SINGLE PARENTING
How to combine bringing up children with your other life goals

Mike Lilley

In the United Kingdom there are now 1.4 million one-parent families, with 2.2 million children – that's one out of five families. There are many routes into single parenthood, all of them difficult to face. However you get there as a single parent, the job of bringing up children alone is very demanding. You have to learn to cope with becoming the only bread-winner in the family as well as taking care of the emotional and physical needs of your children. This book offers some practical ways to ease the hard road of single parenting. It will not take away the isolation and loneliness but it will provide a checklist of the problems you may face and provide ways to overcome them whether emotional, financial, or legal. Mike Lilley is a single parent of three children and a leading spokesperson on the issue of one parent families, appearing regularly on TV and radio. He founded and edited the first national newsstand magazine for single parents *Singled Out*.

160pp. illus. 1 85703 302 7.

MAXIMISING YOUR MEMORY
How to train yourself to remember more

Peter Marshall

A powerful memory brings obvious advantages in educational, career and social terms. At school and college those certificates which provide a passport to a career depend heavily on what you can remember in the exam room. In the world of work, being able to recall details which slip the minds of colleagues will give you a competitive edge. In addition, one of the secrets of being popular with customers and friends is to remember their names and the little things which make them feel they matter to you. This book explains clearly how you can maximise your memory in order to achieve your academic, professional and personal goals. Peter Marshall is a member of the Applied Psychology Research Group of the University of London and works primarily on research into superior memory. He recently assisted with the production of Channel 4's Amazing Memory Show. He is also author of *How To Study and Learn* in this series.

128pp. illus. 1 85703 234 9.

MANAGING YOUR PERSONAL FINANCES
How to achieve financial security and survive the shrinking welfare state

John Claxton

Life for most people has become increasingly troubled by financial worries, both at home and at work, whilst the once dependable welfare state is shrinking. Today's financial world is a veritable jungle full of predators after your money. This book, now revised and updated, will help you to prepare a strategy towards creating your own financial independence. Find out in simple language: how to avoid debt, how to prepare for possible incapacity or redundancy, and how to finance your retirement, including care in old age. Discover how to acquire new financial skills, increase your income, reduce outgoings, and prepare to survive in a more self-reliant world. John Claxton is a Chartered Management Accountant and Chartered Secretary. He teaches personal money management in adult education.

160pp. illus. 1 85703 254 3. 2nd edition

BECOMING A FATHER
How to make a success of your role as a parent

Mike Lilley

The importance of the father as a parent and role model for the child is becoming better recognised today, and fathers themselves have become much more interested in understanding and playing their role. Increasing numbers of fathers are also finding themselves faced with single parenting. But whatever your personal circumstances, this book provides a really practical framework to making a success of fatherhood, from pregnancy and birth to the period of infancy and beyond. Using helpful examples and case studies the book tackles such issues as single fatherhood, the loss of a partner, financial and legal aspects of parenting, child care, juggling domestic and career responsibilities and much more. Mike Lilley is a single father of three children. He edited the magazine *Singled Out*, and has written and broadcast widely on parenting issues. He is also author of *Successful Single Parenting* in this series. He lives in Lichfield, Staffordshire.

128pp. illus. 1 85703 327 2.

CHOOSING A PACKAGE HOLIDAY
How to plan and prepare for a disaster-free experience

Christine Miller

Whether you are going abroad for the first time or are an experienced traveller, this book provides valuable and unbiased information on all aspects of package holidays. By being well briefed before entering the travel agency, you will get the most out of your travel agent and ultimately your holiday. This book shows you how to prepare step-by-step. It guides you through the minefield of: choosing and booking a holiday, taking out appropriate insurance cover, sorting out car hire, obtaining passports and foreign currency, dealing effectively with problems and complaints, and making insurance claims if things go wrong. Do you actually stand to gain anything from special offers and agents' discounts? These and many other subjects are covered to help you make the right holiday choices. Christine Miller has 11 years' experience of working in travel agencies and dealing with all aspects of package holidays. She has travelled extensively both in Europe and worldwide.

144pp. illus. 1 85703 332 9.

HOW TO CLAIM STATE BENEFITS
A practical guide for claimants and advisers

Martin Rathfelder

The Welfare State changes all the time. The third edition of this book has been completely rewritten to take full account of the abolition of the poll tax, mobility allowance, invalidity benefit and unemployment benefit, and the introduction of council tax, disability living allowance, incapacity benefit and jobseeker's allowance – as well as many minor changes. It is the only popular paperback which explains the whole range of benefits available from local and central government, showing you exactly how to claim, and how to arrange your affairs to take advantage of the current benefit system.

160pp illus. 1 85703 073 7. 3rd edition.

HAVING A BABY
How to prepare for and manage pregnancy and the birth of your baby

Dr Stavia Blunt

Having a baby is one of the most physically and emotionally demanding tasks that a woman will ever undertake. A good understanding of what pregnancy and the birth of a child involves is the only way of making informed decisions for yourself. This book is a step-by-step guide taking you from the decision to have a baby, through to conception, pregnancy and delivery of the baby, and finally into the early post-natal period. The contents include: deciding to have a baby, getting pregnant, discovering you are pregnant, recognising changes in pregnancy, monitoring your pregnancy, caring for yourself and your baby during pregnancy, managing problems in pregnancy, preparing for labour, going into labour, getting through labour, discovering your baby, and returning to the non-pregnant state. Dr Stavia Blunt is a consultant physician at a London teaching hospital, and mother of two young children.

160pp. illus. 1 85703 348 5.

RAISING THE SUCCESSFUL CHILD
How to encourage your child on the road to emotional and learning competence

Sylvia Clare

Success comes in many shapes and forms, and goals imposed from external sources, even from a beloved parent, have limited intrinsic value to the child. The more a child is freed from external expectations, the more likely he or she is to succeed within his or her own terms of reference. This book helps parents to examine their own emotions and experiences through a series of exercises, and will deepen their understanding of themselves and their child. The book includes three children's stories, to be read aloud, which will allow the child to interpret his or her world, understand how to face difficult situations and how to address learning opportunities. Sylvia Clare has 16 years' experience as a teacher of psychology and child development. She is also a parent, foster parent and therapist.

144pp. illus. 1 85703 353 1.